PATCHWORK POSSIBILITIES

by
MARJORIE PUCKETT

contents

introduction

getting started

ii

pieced work

applique

patterns

iii

quilting

finishing techniques

introduction

Patchwork . . . a mess or success, both are possibilities.

The purpose of this book is to help quiltmakers of all levels achieve success. As a manual of instruction and patterns, it is designed to assist and guide the novice beginning on a first project, the quiltmaker who is looking for refinement, or the instructor searching for more successful teaching ideas.

Too often a quiltmaker is disappointed as her blocks begin to multiply. She realizes her choice of fabrics needs improving. Sometimes there is just a gradual, growing uneasiness that she is creating a large, king-sized error.

What began as an exciting possibility slowly changes into a necessary obligation to complete. The quiltmaker begins to rationalize there is no longer time for this project. She feels guilty about the wasted time and energy and the needless expense. Even looking at the project makes her feel uncomfortable. The completed blocks and stacks of fabric shift from the sewing area to the closet, then travel to the rafters in the garage or the depths of the basement. She has moved it out of sight but usually not totally out of her mind.

On the other hand, when the techniques of patchwork are understood and applied, the possibilities for patchwork are endless. These techniques include creative designing, precise piecing, and accurate sewing skill.

The power that success has on a quiltmaker is exciting! Executing something well in fabric seems to release unsuspected creativity.

Most of the quilts pictured in this book were 'firsts.' These quiltmakers started by selecting patterns from the book's beginning block category. Then they tried one from the intermediate group, a curved seam block, one with set-in corners, and so forth. Each time, they followed the suggested procedures, explained and illustrated for that technique. As they learned to visualize how fabric's color and print can alter a finished design and perfected their sewing techniques, their feelings of success increased.

This served as a stimulus to each of them to design a sampler quilt, or wall quilt, using their blocks. Notice that some of the samplers consist of four blocks; some are made from six blocks and others total nine or more blocks. Each quiltmaker put her top together using the lattice and border patterns in this text. All of these were designed to fit the book's selection of forty 12-in. (30,5cm) block patterns. Variations of the lattice and border patterns in addition to her own quilting design allowed each quiltmaker to have her own individualized, finished wall quilt.

Patchwork possibilities are infinite, once there is a feeling of success!

Joan Littlefield and Marjorie Puckett

Batting. Cotton or polyester batting comes in a variety of weights and thicknesses and is available by the running yard or in large pre-cut quilt sizes. I only use bonded battings, or those that hold in a tight sheet when pulled. These have less tendency to shift, lump, or migrate within the finished piece. I also prefer thin batts, as quilting stitches will be smaller and are less likely to snag.

Dressmaker's Beeswax. Pulling your hand sewing thread over the surface of this wax will help prevent tangling and keep the thread clean.

Dressmaker's Carbon Paper. Use only the brands that can be removed with a warm iron, or that will wash out of your fabric. Test all brands first.

Eraser. A 'pink' or art gum eraser works best for cleaning up your pencil sketches or tracings.

Fabric. See page 4.

Fabric Marking Pens. Use only those with a water base ink. These completely disappear when wiped with a damp cloth.

Felt-tipped Pen. I keep several red and black fine pointed felt-tipped pens in my supply box. Their dark ink makes a pattern easy to trace. Do not use these pens on fabric.

Glue Stick. A thick stick of glue that comes in a tube just like lipstick. Excellent for temporarily holding appliques in place.

Graph Paper. Buy several pads with four grids to the inch (6mm). Necessary when tracing patterns and great for drawing or sketching.

Iron and Ironing Board.

Masking Tape. Use ¼-in. (6mm) to space rows of quilting and 1-in. (2,5cm) wide roll to aid in tracing patterns, marking rulers, and your sewing machine.

Needles. The higher the number, the smaller the needle. Buy the best quality available, as their cost is low but a needle can really vary in performance. Good needles will also make your stitches look better. Purchase one package each of the following: (1) 'betweens' or 'quilting' for handquilting, size 8 or 10, (2) 'sharps' for hand piecing or applique, size 8, and (3) 'embroidery' in assorted sizes for adding embroidery.

Pencils. Keep several no. 2 lead pencils. Good for sketching, recording information, marking seams or quilting lines on fabric. Several no. 2 white artist's coloring pencils will help make marking on dark fabrics easier.

Pencil Sharpener. A small, hand-held sharpener is more convenient than a surface mounted sharpener. Use it to keep your pencil points sharp and pointed.

Pins, Pin Cushion. Glass-headed dressmaker's pins cost a little more, but they are easier to spot in fabric and the rug so you lose fewer. Try to find those with white heads, about 1½ (3,8cm) long.

Quilter's Tote. This indispensable accessory holds everything needed for the 'quilter on the go.' It has slots for pencils, marking pens, ruler, and quilter's guides. The sewing kit and pin cushion easily snap out. There are pockets to hold patterns, graph and notebook paper, even your favorite patchwork books. One large pocket holds the wide assortment of fabrics you'll want to carry with you. You can make your own quilter's tote using Simplicity pattern 5311.

Quilting Frame or Hoop. This tool holds your layers taut during hand quilting. A floor frame takes up a lot of space, isn't portable, but can accommodate many people quilting at one time. A hoop, by contrast, is portable, easy to tuck away, but only one person can work at a time. An ideal hoop should be 23 to 24 in. (58-61 cm).

Rubber Balloon, Disk, or Gripper. Keep one or the other in your supplies to grasp stubborn needles that won't pull through heavy or thick fabric.

Rubber Cement. A paper working glue used in making templates from graph paper and sandpaper.

Rulers. I would suggest two rulers—a 6-in. (16cm) clear see-through plastic ruler for marking seam allowance and a 12-in. (30,5cm) or 18-in. (45,5cm) for drawing straight lines.

Safety Pins. Rust proof, size 2 safety pins are great for pin basting layers of a quilt together when quilting without a frame.

Sandpaper. Keep four or five sheets of stiff, medium grit sandpaper on hand to use as a work surface and from which to make templates. Fabric won't slip when placed against sandpaper.

Scissors. Three different pairs are needed—(1) old or dull scissors for cutting paper and sandpaper, (2) sharp fabric cutting scissors, and (3) a small pair of embroidery scissors to trim threads and fabric ends.

Sewing Machine. Many patchwork patterns need to be assembled by hand, but there is also good opportunity to use the machine.

Thimble. A properly fitted thimble will prevent sore fingers. Practice with it before you begin hand sewing patchwork.

Thread. Always use the best thread available as your finished project will only be as strong as the thread you put into it. Choose colors that blend with the predominant tone of fabrics when piecing shapes together. For hand or machine sewing I use a cotton or cotton/polyester. Quilting thread is a heavier thread and is pre-waxed. I find it difficult to hand piece with this, so I use it for quilting only.

color

terms and principles

A brief review of the terms commonly used when discussing color can improve your ability to enjoy and utilize patchwork. Everyone can acquire expertise in choosing the right colors and gain the ability to combine prints in an interesting way. You will become more confident if you understand the principles of color, then experiment and practice with fabrics.

There are three **primary colors or hues.** ● They are called primaries because they are the basic colors and are not made by mixing other colors.

When two primary colors are mixed together, **secondary colors** ■ are produced.

Colors obtained from mixing a primary and a secondary color are called **intermediates.** ▲ The three primaries, the three secondaries, and the six intermediates comprise the twelve pure colors or hues on a color wheel.

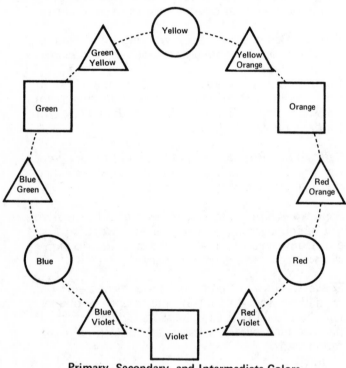

Primary, Secondary, and Intermediate Colors

color intensity

Every color has intensity or strength or purity. Intensity is different from the tint or shade of a color, which is the amount of white or black added to a pure color. The intensity of color is changed when varying amounts of gray are added to it. Intensity can range from bright to dull depending on how much gray is added.

Intense colors can be added to part of a quilt's lattice or border giving needed snap or zing to the composition. Small amounts of intense color will also impart character when large areas of that tint is present.

texture influences color

Texture plays an important part in color. A fabric with a rough texture reflects light in tiny accents, throwing little shadows that dull the intensity of the fabric's true color. A bright red dye applied to a textured fabric will appear mellowed, while the same dye applied to a smooth, shiny fabric will have a harsh and glaring effect.

Printed fabrics give the feeling of surface texture. Because they have a foreground and a background, a feeling of depth is created. Solid colored fabrics, in contrast, will appear flat and their colors more intense. Quilting can add softness and depth to these fabrics.

solving a color problem

All the color principles should be regarded as flexible. Everyone's sensitivity and taste in color is different. Your ability to combine fabrics skillfully will improve with study and work. You will find yourself adding new combinations to your mental file, and discarding others, as you allow your intuitive or spontaneous feelings to surface. The following are techniques to train your mind and your eyes to observe color.

Tune into your negative responses. Why is that color unattractive to you? Why don't you like it? We are often unaware of why we like something, but forget to ask about the opposite reaction.

When combining many fabrics, study them in the proportion in which they will be used. Don't work with a large piece of red fabric when you are thinking of using only a small amount of red. Fold the red, or cut out sections of it, in proportion to the finished project.

Squint at your selection. Is your composition bland? Do you need more variety, a pinch of spice, such as a contrasting color, or more intense colors? Perhaps some of the fabrics you've added aren't working but instead, fight with what you had in mind. Adapt the fabrics as necessary as your design develops. One fabric isn't all important. Manipulate your collection of fabrics to make its fullest statement.

View your proposed block or pattern in the room or area where the finished quilt will be enjoyed. Remember how outside sources can influence color. The size of a room, natural vs. artificial lighting, color cast from a large or dominating carpet, or the colors of the walls will all effect the colors in your quilt.

If you don't know where the quilt will be used, try to work over a large cream or beige sheet or piece of muslin. You'll get a truer feeling of how the colors influence each other than if you work over a bright green carpet, or on the yellow linoleum kitchen floor.

Don't be afraid to make a mistake, you may create something new!

color harmonies

Colors that go well together, creating an underlying sense of order, make a color harmony or color scheme. Over the years artisans have developed standard color harmonies which can serve as a framework upon which to build, and will carry you along to color combinations which might otherwise be overlooked. Color harmonies can also serve to stimulate your imagination.

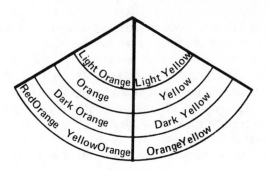

An Analogous Color Harmony

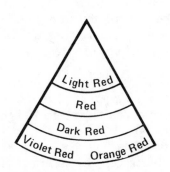

A Monochromatic Color Harmony

Monochromatic harmonies use one, single color. Small rooms or enclosed areas can appear larger when quilts or wall hangings using monochromatic harmonies are placed in them. One-color harmonies usually appear soothing to the eye, but this does not mean that they will be boring or without variation. Terry Hedani's wall quilt on page 46 and the sampler quilt by Mary Lou Crossett on page 47 prove this point.

Using one color, such as red, for a monochromatic scheme means you could also include all its different values, shades, tints, and intensities. You could use bright red, ruby red, dark red, burnt brick red, Indian red, watermelon red, light fuchsia, bright pink, light pink, gray pink, etc. Study the amount and range of rusts that Mary Lou incorporated into her sampler.

Additional interest can be added to a monochromatic harmony if there is contrast in textures. Try combining smooth, shiny cotton sateen with linen, organdy, velvet, satin, homespun cotton duck or silk shantung. Observe the textures Lynn Connell used in her green blocks shown on page 48.

Neutral colors can always be added to any harmony. When joined with a monochromatic scheme, neutrals help stretch your one color making it less necessary to purchase huge varieties of that color. Lisa Taylor used large quantities of neutrals or creams in her sampler shown on page 45. Notice that she also took advantage of the right and wrong sides of a fabric. This is another way to extend what may look like a limited selection of one color. The wrong side of a fabric will automatically blend with its right side since it is a lighter tint of the same color.

An **analogous color harmony** is based on two to four colors that lay next to each other on the color wheel. They are usually most agreeable when they are limited to those colors falling between the primaries, and may include any or all of the adjacent hues. A good analogous harmony shows one underlying color throughout the harmony.

Roxie Sue's sampler quilt on page 52 is based on an analogous harmony through the use of blue, blue-violet, violet, and red-violet. Notice that most of the blue is introduced in the lattice.

3

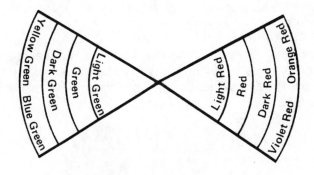

A Complementary Color Harmony

Complementary harmonies are made from two colors directly opposite each other on the color wheel. Combinations of opposite colors are more difficult to use than those of neighboring colors. When they are done well, however, they are richer than related harmonies and more satisfying to the eye. The addition of a contrasting color to a color scheme is like adding pepper to food, it has to be added with care, and sampled along the way. You will discover that complementary colors placed side by side make each other look brighter. Green will look greener next to red, and red will look brighter next to green.

Lynn McBratney's sampler on page 51 and Lynn Connell's quilt on page 48 are both complementary harmonies, but done with fabric with differing green intensities and pieces varying in size.

Because complementary colors visually intensify each other, you may want to purposely select complements for a project that will 'jump out' or make a strong visual statement.

hints on prints

Understanding how to use prints in patchwork is equally as important as understanding color. Try to get a mixture of prints—small florals, tiny dots, flowing, swirling prints and even stripes. I divide prints into five categories. The sampler quilt will explode with beauty and be uniquely different if you design actively with these groupings.

Background prints are usually soft and subtle in color; they often appear to be a solid color from a distance.

Small prints are useful for the tinier areas of a design and are available in both regular or irregular print placement. Try to have some of both. Stay away from prints comprised of many colors; prints with two shades of one color are preferable.

Medium sized prints with regular or irregular design placement are another must in your fabric collection. I tend to avoid fabrics with stark white backgrounds or with closely spaced, regularly repeating designs such as polka dots or checks. These kinds of patterns 'stick out' and never quite blend with the other prints.

Large prints such as paisleys, chintzes, and large florals often contain many colors and will need to be used with discretion. You can position your templates over these fabrics to cut out just the area or design you desire.

Dark prints or fabrics heavily saturated with color are vital to your mixture. These fabrics have the ability to pull your total design together. Avoid prints with extra busy designs or those that combine many colors.

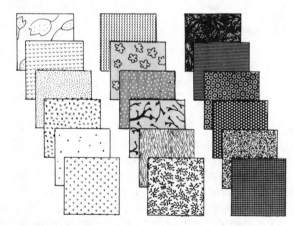

fabric selection

Always buy the best quality fabric you can afford. Your finished quilt or wall quilt will only be as good as your weakest fabric.

When shopping for fabric, try to find yardages that look and feel similar to the fabrics found in pillowcases or sheets; these will be broadcloth weight. Look for 'woven' fabrics with a high cotton content as such fabrics tend to have a better 'hand' or 'feel.' They should feel soft to the touch but not limp or sheer like voile or organza. Fabrics like these will fray too

easily. Avoid stiff or rigid material like denim or canvas or fabrics heavy with sizing. Read the label on the bolt to be sure the yardage is pre-shrunk and colorfast. Avoid knits, velvet or velveteen, corduroy and satins. These types of fabric tend to stretch, ravel easily, are bulky or slide around making it hard for a beginner to work with them.

how much to buy

For a sampler wall quilt, I advise purchasing 3/8 yard (0.3 meter) cuts of 20 to 30 different fabrics.

Plan to execute your quilt using one of the color harmonies discussed on page 3. This means your sampler would be constructed from one or two main colors. You may include pure hues, shades, and tints of the color, and a variety of intensities in these one or two families.

Purchase 7 to 10 fabrics that are dark shades of these colors and in a variety of print mixtures. Select 7 to 10 medium colors and also 7 to 10 light colors in the same manner.

Purchase an additional 5 fabrics in a complimentary color or fabric that accent or contrast. These might appear contrasting because they are bold and intense or soft and light.

prepare and store fabrics

I put all new purchased yardage directly into the washer and dryer as soon as I get home with it. I don't want to accidentally place it in my stock of yardage only to have it shrink or bleed after it is sewn into a design. I separate the dark fabrics from the light fabrics and wash them in hot soapy water. Laundering will remove the excess sizing and loose color while relaxing the fibers. If a yardage shows excessive wrinkles when removed from the dryer, I won't put it into my fabric collection. Any quilted patchwork, especially a quilt, is never pressed as the iron's heat and weight will flatten the loft of the batting.

I store my fabrics according to color in large, clear plastic sweater or blanket boxes. Because I purchase many fabrics planning to use the wrong side rather than the right side, I fold each yardage with the side showing that originally attracted me to it.

Once I've gathered fabrics for a project, they are kept together in my tote or a basket so that I'm constantly designing from that stack or collection. I like samplers made with many fabrics, but once I've selected 20 to 30 fabrics for a new design, I draw from that stack so the finished product has continuity. Of course, occasionally a few new fabrics may need to be introduced to this collection. Once you start cutting and designing, you usually discover that, to your dismay, there are some fabrics that don't have the potential you thought they might. Remove them from your collection and return them to storage.

making template

Place a sheet of graph paper over the pattern you have chosen. Using a sharp pencil and ruler, trace each shape accurately. Add the grain line, letter of the alphabet and all other information given with each shape.

Glue the graph paper to the smooth side of a sheet of sandpaper using rubber cement. Do not use white glue.

Using old scissors, cut out the templates carefully, just a hair's width to the inside of your pencil line.

tracing onto fabric

Stop and check the accuracy of your templates by placing them over the originals in this book. Trim as necessary or the finished blocks may be too large.

Tape large sheets of sandpaper to your tabletop, rough sides facing up. Your fabric will adhere to this surface, eliminating the problems of shifting or scooting when tracing around the templates. Place the fabric, wrong side facing up, over the sandpaper work surface. Position the first template onto the fabric, with the template's grain lines even with those of the fabric.

template placed off-grain

The lengthwise grain runs parallel to the fabric's selvage while the cross grain runs perpendicular, or in the same direction, as the fabric's cut ends. The template shown does not match the cross grain or lengthwise grain, so it is incorrectly placed.

shape drawn on fabric

By pivoting the template you can easily see when its marked grain line matches those of the yardage. This shows how the template should have been positioned.

When tracing around the templates, use a no. 2 lead pencil on light colored fabrics and a no. 2 artist's white pencil on dark fabrics. Keep the pencil sharpened to a fine point because a rounded or thick point will enlarge your shape and cause problems later. Trace with short, stroking motions rather than dragging the pencil around the template and distorting the fabric beneath.

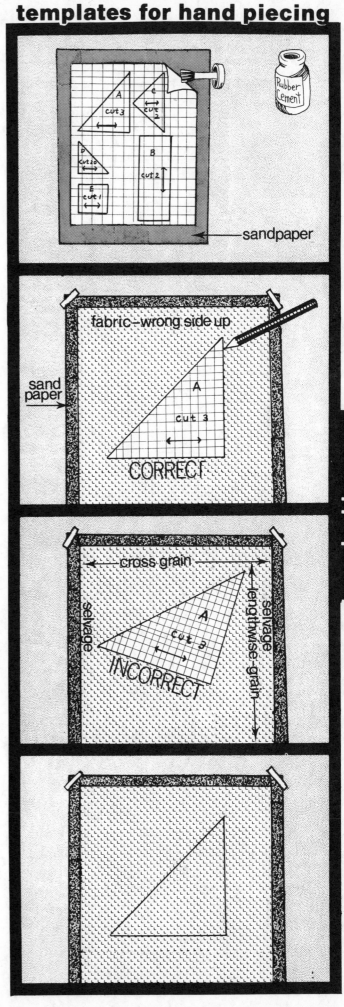

5

pieced work and applique

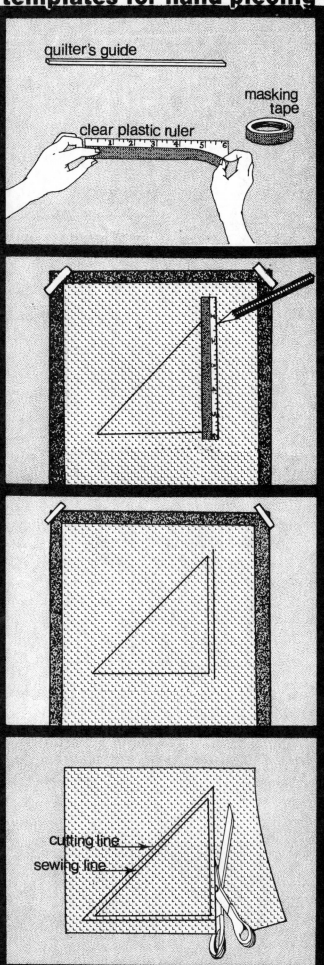

6

tools for seam allowance

Seam allowance must be added to each shape as drawn. The standard seam for hand sewing is ¼ in. (6mm). A clear plastic 6-in. (15cm) ruler is the best tool for quickly adding seam allowances. Place a strip of masking tape across the ruler's surface, ¼ in. (6mm) from its edge. A quilter's guide or short plastic bar can also be used.

You will be able to eyeball a ¼-in. (6mm) seam allowance after some practice but use either of these tools for your first blocks.

adding seam allowance

When using the prepared ruler for adding seam allowance, place it over your fabric, matching the edge of the tape on the ruler with the pencil line drawn on the fabric. Trace along the edge of the extended ruler to add your seam allowance. If using a quilter's guide, place it to the outside of the pencil lines of the shape.

one seam allowance drawn

Seam allowance has been added to one edge of this shape. Now add seam allowance to the remaining sides.

cutting out shape

When seam allowance has been added to all sides, cut the shape out using the second or cutting line.

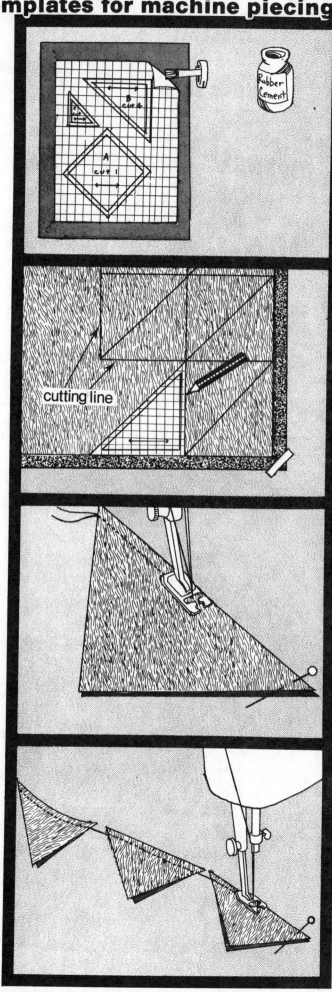

making template

If you plan to machine assemble your patchwork, the templates need to be constructed with a built-in seam allowance. To do this, place a sheet of graph paper over the pattern you have chosen. Trace one shape at a time, adding the ¼ in. (6mm) to the pattern. Mark and letter the templates as you would for hand piecing.

Prepare sandpaper templates as described on page 5.

clustering shapes

Place your yardage over a sandpaper work surface as you would for hand piecing. Position the template onto the wrong side of the yardage keeping the grain lines in mind. Using a sharp, fine pointed pencil, trace around the shape, aligning the edges of each new tracing with the previously drawn pencil line. This one line will be your cutting line.

use presser foot for seam allowance

When machine sewing, the pieces are facing right sides together and held with pins placed perpendicular to the seam.

The width from the center to the right edge of the presser foot on many machines will be ¼ in. (6mm). You can use this to establish your seam allowance.

Also, use the etched seam guide on the plate beneath the presser foot or place masking tape across the plate ¼ in. (6mm) from where the needle goes into the bobbin case.

machine chain feeding

Chain feed your work through the machine using 12 to 14 stitches per running inch (2,5cm), without cutting the units apart. There is no need to begin or end each unit with backstitching.

Machine piecing or assemblying is fast but not all patterns can be machine sewn. I encourage beginners to learn hand piecing first, then try a pattern on the machine. With experience you will learn when to hand or machine piece. Some patterns can be done successfully by combining both techniques.

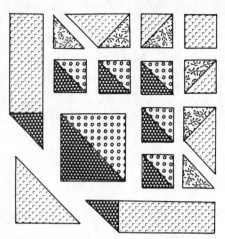

Diagram 1—Sew small pieces to make larger units of squares or blocks.

8

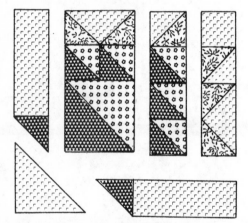

Diagram 2—Join the squares or pieces to form long units, rows, or strips.

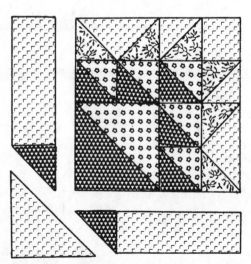

Diagram 3—Sew forming seams as long as possible.

An instruction sheet is always included with dressmaker patterns, giving detailed drawings and instructions on how to assemble that particular garment or item. Patchwork patterns also require a step-by-step procedure for assemblying. With practice and by studying every pattern before you start to sew it together, you can avoid problems or mistakes.

I always lay the total design or block out in front of me before and while I'm assemblying it. This allows me to decide which pieces to join together first, and also eliminates the chances of picking up two correct pieces but sewing the wrong edges together. This can happen if you stack your work instead of laying it back down in its correct position.

Simplicity Pattern 5311 has a Quilter's Tote which includes patterns for large squares of felt. These are used like a flannel board. You can see your fabric patches against a contrasting color of felt and your fabrics will also adhere to the felt rather than slipping. The felt squares can be rolled, securely tied, and placed back in the Quilter's Tote until you have time to resume stitching.

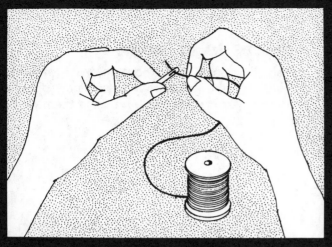

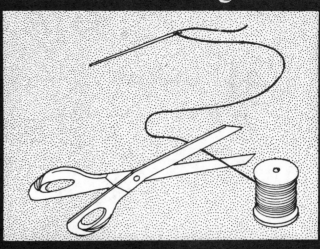

thread needle

Cut across the tip of your thread at an angle and thread this end through your needle. Use a 'sharp' size 8 or 10 for hand sewing.

cut thread loose

Cut a thread strand no longer than 18 in. (46cm). This is about the same length as the distance from your fingertips to your elbow.

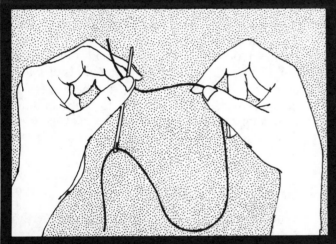

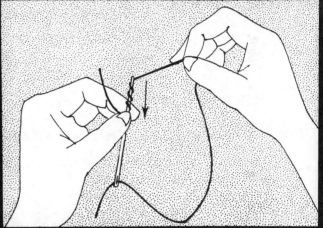

knot with spool-cut end

To make a knot in your thread, use the cut end from the spool. Place this end between your fingertips and the needle.

three wraps

Wrap the thread three or four times around the needle while holding the cut end between the fingers and the needle. Pull downward.

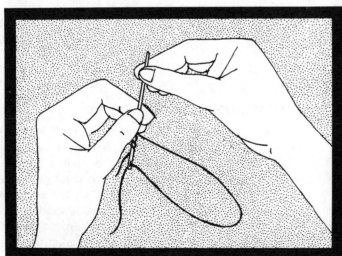

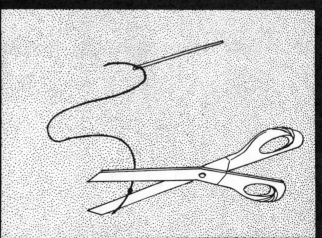

slide wraps off

While pinching the wraps, pull the needle up with your free hand. A knot will form near the tail of the thread.

trim end.

Trim away any excess thread resting behind the knot.

pieced work and applique

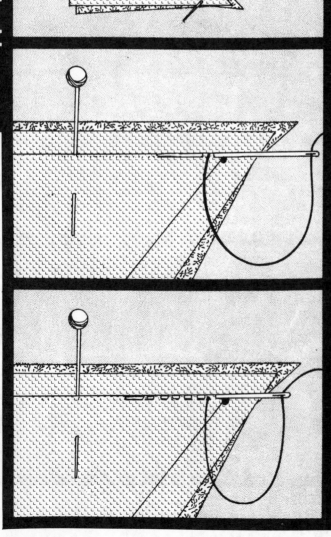

pieces to be sewn

Place the entire block out in front of you. After reviewing the assemblying sequence discussed on page 8, join two pieces by placing them right sides together.

correct placement of pins

Notice that the penciled sewing lines are visible because you drew them onto the wrong side of the material. Insert a pin into the far right corner where the pencil lines come together. Check the back side to see that the pin is extending from the same corresponding position. Place the next pin into the left corner in a similar manner. One pin is usually needed along the middle line. Check the back sides also. All pins are placed perpendicular to the seam line. Additional pins may be added if the seam is longer than 4 or 5 in. (10 or 12,5 cm) or if it has a bias edge.

begin at marked corner

Begin sewing by taking a backstitch exactly at the corner pin. Right handed people will sew from right to left, and left handed people will work from left to right.

hand sewing seams

Proceed with a running stitch until the needle is loaded. The stitching should be just a hair's width inside the pencil line. Check the back side of your work frequently to see that your sewing runs along the back pencil line. You will be able to load your needle with three to eight stitches depending on the thickness of the fabrics. Each time you start stitching or loading your needle take a small backstitch.

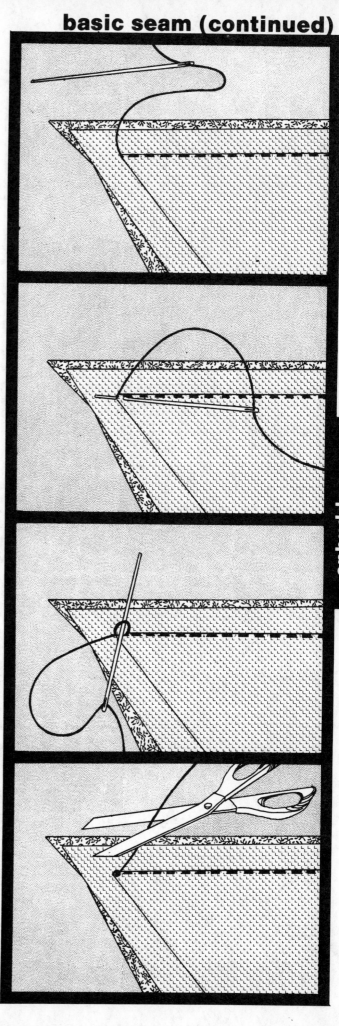

ending seam

Try to average 8 to 10 stitches per running inch, removing all pins as you reach them. Hand stitching will feel awkward at first but in a short while you will feel more confident. You will work faster and your stitches will be more evenly spaced. Bring the needle up at the last pin or where the pencil lines come together.

backstitching

Take a small backstitch, sewing always on or slightly below the stitching line.

making knot

Slip your needle through the loop that has been formed by the backstitch and pull the loop closed. You may want to do this twice.

trim thread

Trim the remaining thread close to the knot. Place the sewn pieces back into position with the other patches and decide which units to assemble next. I usually press all seams after the block is assembled but this will be determined by the block itself. Seams are always pressed together, not open as in dressmaking. Press the seam toward the darkest fabric or away from the bulk where other seams meet. Use gentle pressure being careful not to stretch the fabric.

I try to press the wrong side of a block first, then press from the right side.

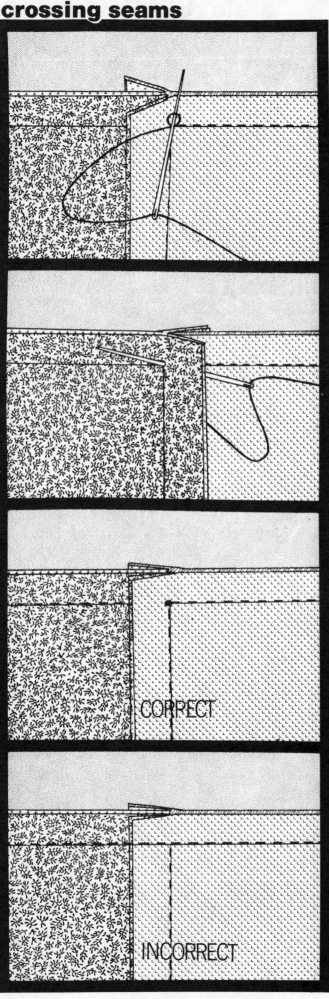

backstitch before crossing seam

When rows are being joined and seams are being crossed, I try to do very accurate pinning. If I don't, the crossing seam will have a sideways step. Rows to be joined are placed right sides together, and pinned at both their corners and along the seam or pencil line. Check the backside to see that the pins are coming through at the same position. Sew to the first crossing seam, stitching just a hair's width below the seam line. Take a small backstitch and slip your needle through the loop, then pull to form a knot.

crossing through seams

Slip the needle through the seam allowance, then finger press it back over the stitched seam. Continue sewing along the stitching line; check the back side frequently to see that the stitches are also on that pencil line.

correct

The seam allowance has not been sewn down but remains free to be pressed to either side.

incorrect

The wrong way to cross seams because the stitching crosses the seam allowance.

finishing block

I classify blocks like Queen of the May and Dusty Miller as circular moving patterns. They dictate their own particular assemblying sequence.

These patterns usually have a circle, square, or hexagon in the center. After the block is pieced, the center can be set in using the set-in corner technique on page 16 or appliqued in place as described on page 20.

two pieces sewn together

Place the entire block out in front of you, then sew two pieces together making a unit. Notice that the stitching is just a hair's width below the seam line and the stitching starts and ends at the pencil line corners.

assembling into units

Place the assembled units back in front of you and decide if they in turn can be sewn into quarters or thirds.
The quarter units are then sewn forming halves.

assembling into halves

Don't be concerned if the block does not divide in half evenly. The procedure is the same even if one unit has seven pieces and the other has eight. If there is a second row of circular moving pieces, they should be assembled in the same manner. Press the seam allowances to one side. The last step is to applique or set in the central circle, square, or hexagon.

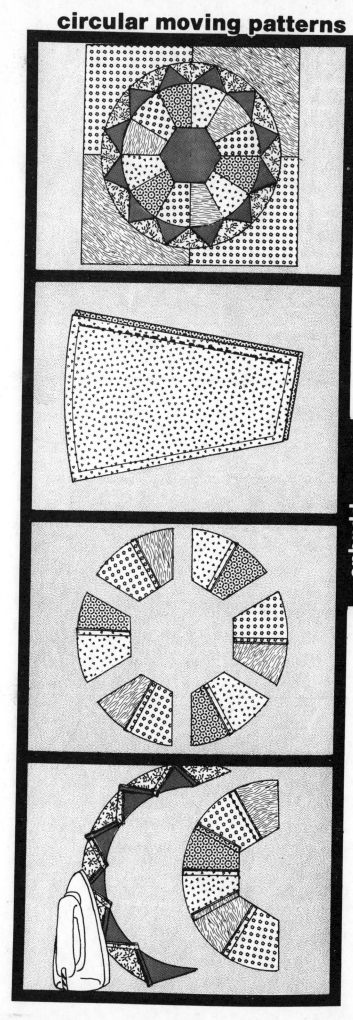

13

pieced work and applique

curved seams

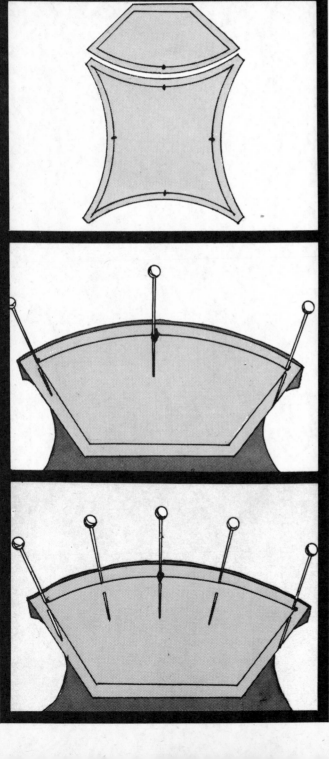

templates for curved seam work

I think some of the most beautiful pieced patterns are curved seam blocks, so four have been included in this book. These patterns are not difficult when you follow the basic piecing steps.

When tracing the patterns, you must include the center mark indicated on each curved seam.

fabrics correctly marked

Place the curved seam pieces out in front of you, wrong side facing up. The penciled sewing lines will be visible along with the center mark.

correct pinning for curved seams

Place the convex curve (outward curve) on top of the concave curve (inward curve). Pin right sides together at the corner pencil lines and at the center mark. Pins must be placed perpendicular to the stitching line. Check the back side of the pieces to see that the pins emerge at the corresponding position.

add more pins as necessary

Additional pins are added as needed to ease the fabric into place.

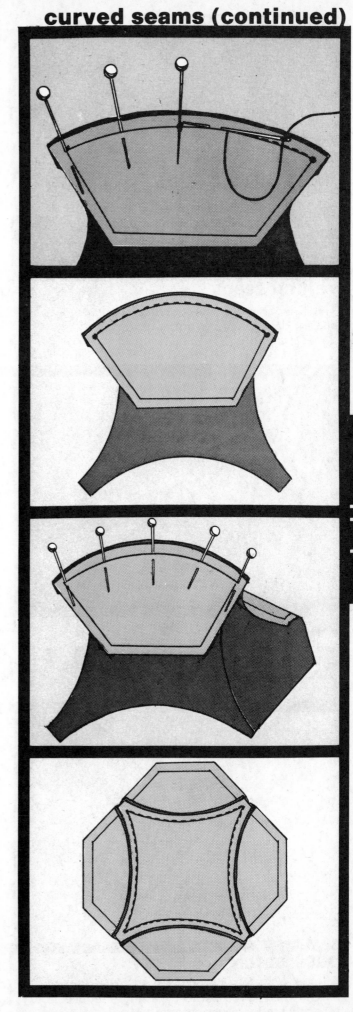

sewing curved seams

Sew the pieces in the usual manner, starting at the first pin or corner where the pencil lines meet. Remove the pins as you sew to them.

completed curved seam

The completed seam will look like this. Notice that the stitching does not extend into the seam allowance.

adding next curved piece

Each additional curved seam piece is pinned and sewn in a similar manner.

curved seams pressed into place

When all the curved seams are sewn, turn your work over and study the back side. The seam allowances will tend to naturally lay to one side or the other. I usually press them to the direction they want to lay. If this causes a shadow on the front, notches or pie-shaped wedges can be cut and the seam allowance pressed in the other direction.

15

pieced work
and applique

set-in corners

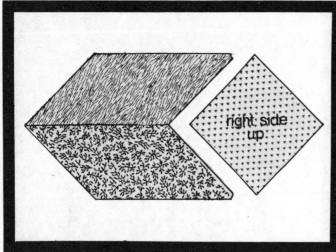

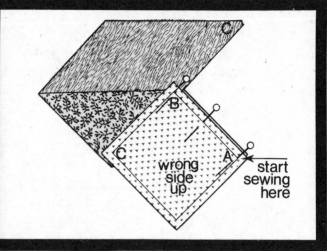

getting ready

This is what a set-in corner looks like before it is pieced. Place the pieces out in front of you, right sides facing up.

pin in place

Position the piece to be set in, right side facing up. Pin at the pencil corners and along the pencil line. Pins should emerge at the same position on the back.

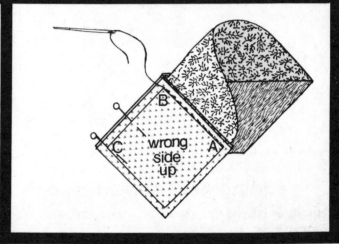

backstitch at corner

Sew from (A) to inside corner (B) where you take a small backstitch, passing the needle through the loop just before the loop closes.

turn, pin remaining seam

Pivot the top patch and pin as shown, starting with far corner (C). Pin along the pencil line halfway across the seam, checking the back side.

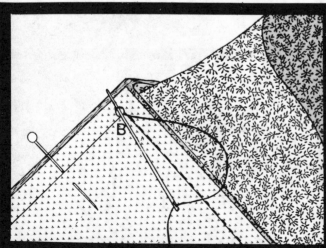

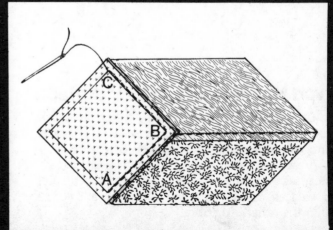

back stitch

As you start to sew from (B) to (C), take one stitch, then a backstitch, passing the needle through the loop just before it is pulled closed.

finishing

Continue sewing to (C), ending with a backstitch and knot (page 11). Press the assembled unit, pressing the seams to one side.

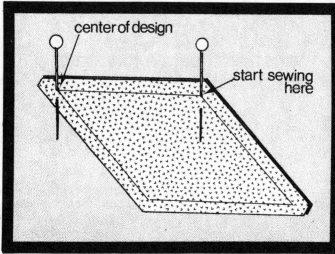

sew toward center of block

When sewing pieces together that will fit into a center, start stitching from the outside edge, working towards the center.

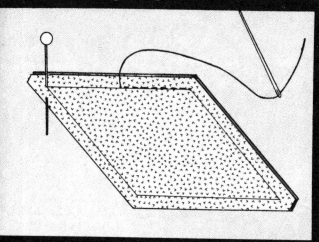

sew halfway

Beginning at the pencil corner, sew halfway across the seam following the pencil lines. Check the back side of your work occasionally.

17

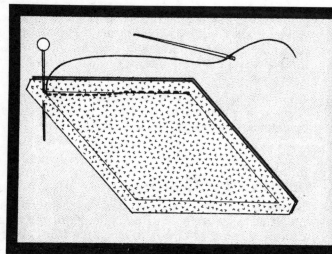

take a deeper seam

Sew the remaining half with a slightly deeper seam allowance, sewing just below the pencil line. End your work at the pencil corners.

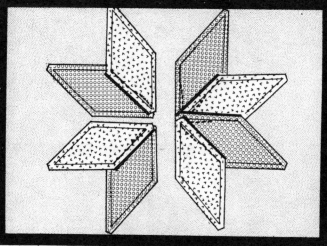

quarters, then halves

Sew the pieces into quarters, then halves, following the same pinning and sewing technique for every seam.

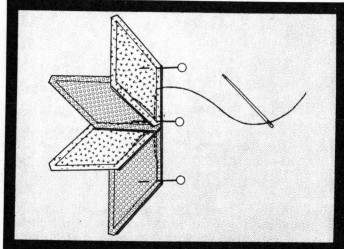

join halves

The seam allowances are pressed to one side. Trim the excess fabric from the points of the pieces and press the center open.

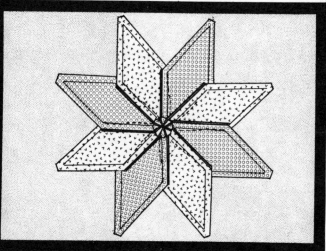

press seams

When sewing halves together, take a deeper seam as you approach and leave the center. Don't stitch down or through the center seam allowances.

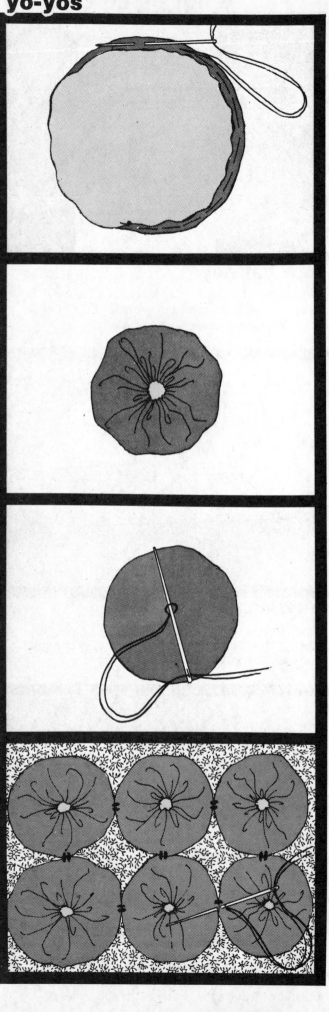

turn back seam allowance

These gathered circular patches are purely for decoration. They have no filler in them and often need to be applied over a backing to add stability. Cut the number of fabric circles required. They should be twice the size of the finished yo-yo plus a ¼-in. (6mm) seam allowance.

Turn a ¼-in. (6mm) hem to the wrong side and by hand make running or basting stitches ¼ in. (6mm) long close to the fold. Keep the stitches even. Use double thread, starting with a knot placed in the fold of the hem.

gathered yo-yo

When you have completely stitched around the circle, pull the thread to close the circle. This causes the fabric to double over on itself. If small stitches were taken, there would be lots of small gathers and the center would not close tightly. When ¼-in. (6mm) stitches are used, the fabric will pleat, allowing for a tighter center.

A contrasting color can be added to each yo-yo by slipping a small piece of fabric into the gathered opening before the gathers are tightly pulled.

fastening off work

Flatten and center the hole, pushing the needle and thread through it to the back side. Knot the thread securely being careful not to catch the front edges of the yo-yo. The gathered, puckered side of the yo-yo with the center hole is the front and the smooth side is the back.

joining yo-yos

Place two yo-yos right sides together and sew with three or four overcasting or whip stitches just catching their folds. Usually they are assembled into horizontal or vertical rows, but sometimes you may want a circular grouping.

Each yo-yo should be tacked down to a background fabric with a stitch in each quarter of the circle edge which will add stability and also give additional color and depth to the design.

applying fabrics to a foundation

Crazy patchwork is decorative and offers the needle-worker an opportunity to combine fabrics of various textures and colors in an original way. Try using scraps of wool, velvets, silks, and even satins!

Cut a foundation fabric from soft, lightweight material. Begin covering the foundation with the decorative fabrics, starting at the top and working across the foundation.

adding more shapes

Cut simple shapes, larger than you want, overlapping them. Pin under the seam allowances; fold the fabrics to make interesting angles and curves. The edges that extend beyond the foundation will be trimmed even with the foundation and sewn into the seam allowance with the block.

finished design

You can choose one of several methods to sew the patches in place. Perhaps you want to machine top-stitch the pieces down, or do a basting stitch by hand. Both of these choices require decorative embroidery added later. If you slip stitch the edges under by hand, you have a number of creative possibilities for decorating your work. You can embroider right over the edges or you can stitch either to the left or right or embroider two rows over a seam.

For the 'corner fan' or 'center fan' patterns given on page 60, ribbon or lace has been used for the spokes and decoration.

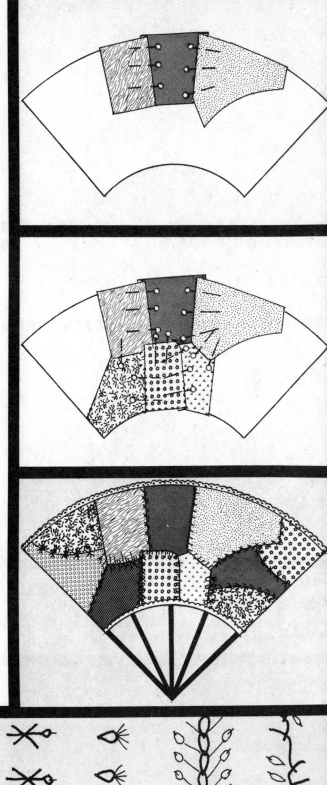

19

pieced work and applique

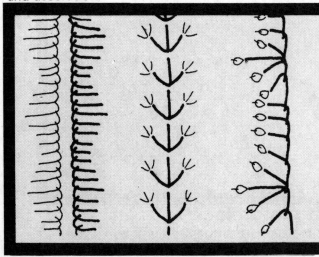

sample of embroidery stitches

basic applique

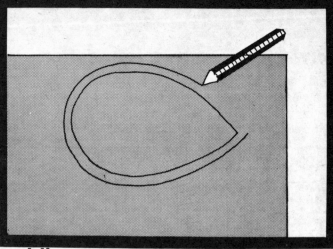

tracing onto fabric
Position the template onto the right side of fabric, tracing lightly around it with a sharp pencil.

adding seam allowance
Drawing freehand, add a ¼-in. (6mm) seam allowance. Cut shape out along outside line.

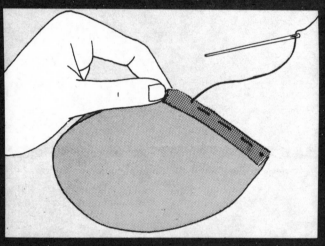

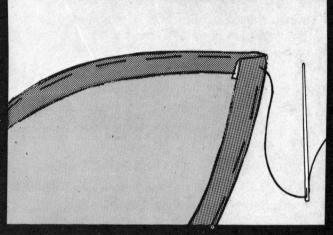

finger pressing & basting seam allowance
Finger press the seam allowance toward the wrong side, basting close to the fold edge.

basting points
If pattern has a sharp point, begin and end at point, basting all the way off the edge.

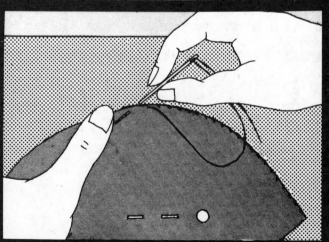

prepare background
Fold and finger crease the background fabric along the diagonals, and through the center horizontally and vertically. Position appliques.

sewing into place
Use one pin for each shape, its points parked to the wrong side and its head firmly against the top. Use a thread that matches the appliques, taking small slip or blind stitches.

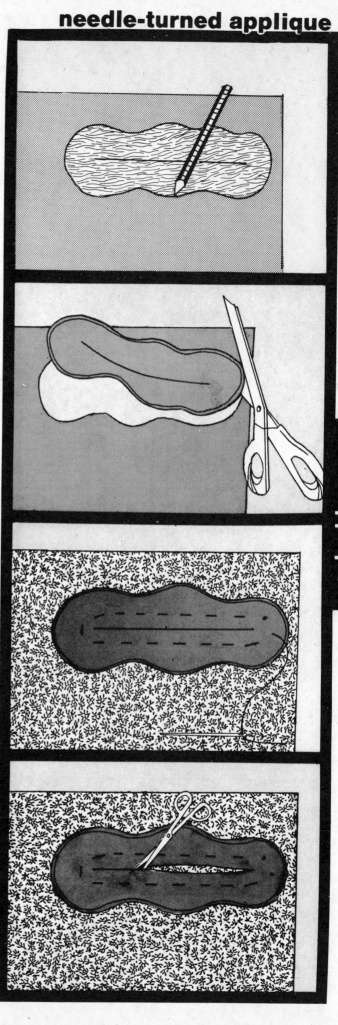

tracing onto fabric

Applique shapes with deep inside curves need to be handled with needle-turned techniques. Trace around each template onto the right side of the fabric. Use a sharp pencil, drawing lightly.

cutting out shapes

Cut the shape out, adding a scant 1/8 in. (3mm) seam allowance as you cut. It is not necessary to draw the cutting line onto the fabric as you did for basic applique.

basting down applique

Fold and finger crease the background fabric along the diagonals and through the center horizontally and vertically as for basic applique. Position and baste appliques down to the background.

cut inside line

Some shapes require needle-turning along their inside as well as along their outside edges. Using the tip of embroidery scissors cut a slit through the basted shape only.

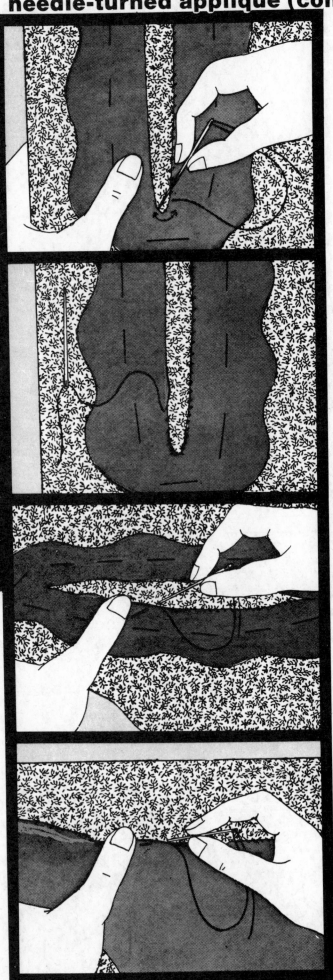

needle-turning under seam allowance

Using the needle as a tool, roll and turn the raw edge of the applique under 1/16 to 1/8 in. (1-1/2 to 3 mm). Hold the turned-under edge with the thumb of your free hand just ahead of your stitching.

correct stitch

This tiny, almost invisible, stitch should be done with thread closely matching the applique pieces. As you sew, pull slightly on your thread to set the stitches snugly into place. This will also help you achieve a smooth line, whether the finished edge is straight or curved.

holding seam allowance down with thumb

The stitches are placed no further than 1/8 in. (3mm) apart. I sew holding the needle-turned edges down with the thumb of my free hand, pinching my work in 1/2 in. (1,3cm) jumps.

Another piece of fabric may be inserted through the center slit to make the inside shape a different color. Be sure the new piece is larger than the slit.

sewing down outside edge

The outside edges of the appliques are needle-turned and sewn in a similar manner. Remove the basting and press gently if necessary once the design is completely sewn.

pieced work and applique

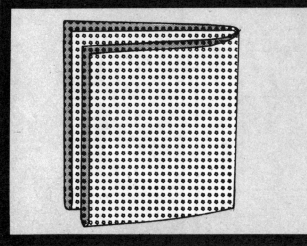

fold fabric

Large background spaces can be broken into flowing areas as shown in the original designs of Tulip Wreath, Ruffled Tulips, and El Modena Rose. First fold selected fabric into fourths.

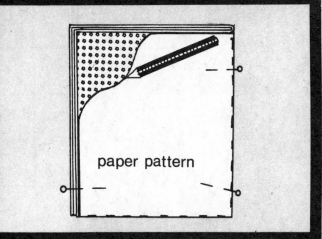

paper pattern

position pattern

Place broken lines of the pattern along double folds. Hold in place with pins. Using a sharp pencil, trace along edge of pattern.

23

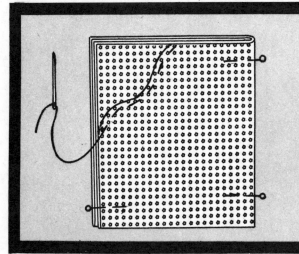

baste through layers

With needle and thread, baste through the four layers, just inside the drawn line.

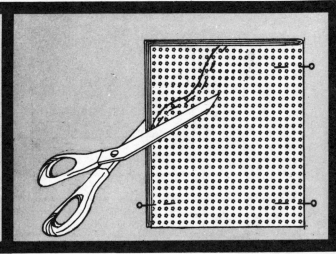

cut layers

Using sharp dressmaker's scissors, cut along pencil line through all four layers. Recut or smooth the edges as necessary until the four layers are exactly the same.

pieced work and applique

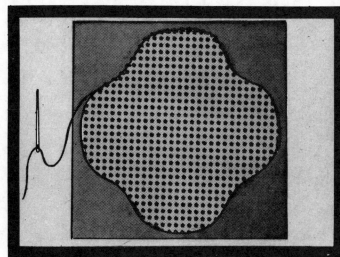

sew shape onto ground fabric

Fasten cut shape onto the ground fabric by basting close to the cut edge. Sew the shape down using needle-turned applique techniques.

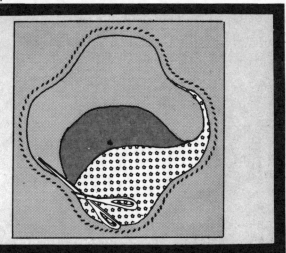

trim ground fabric behind shape

Carefully trim out ground fabric from behind, leaving ¼ in. (6mm) seam allowance. This eliminates fabric bulk and shadowing from ground fabric.

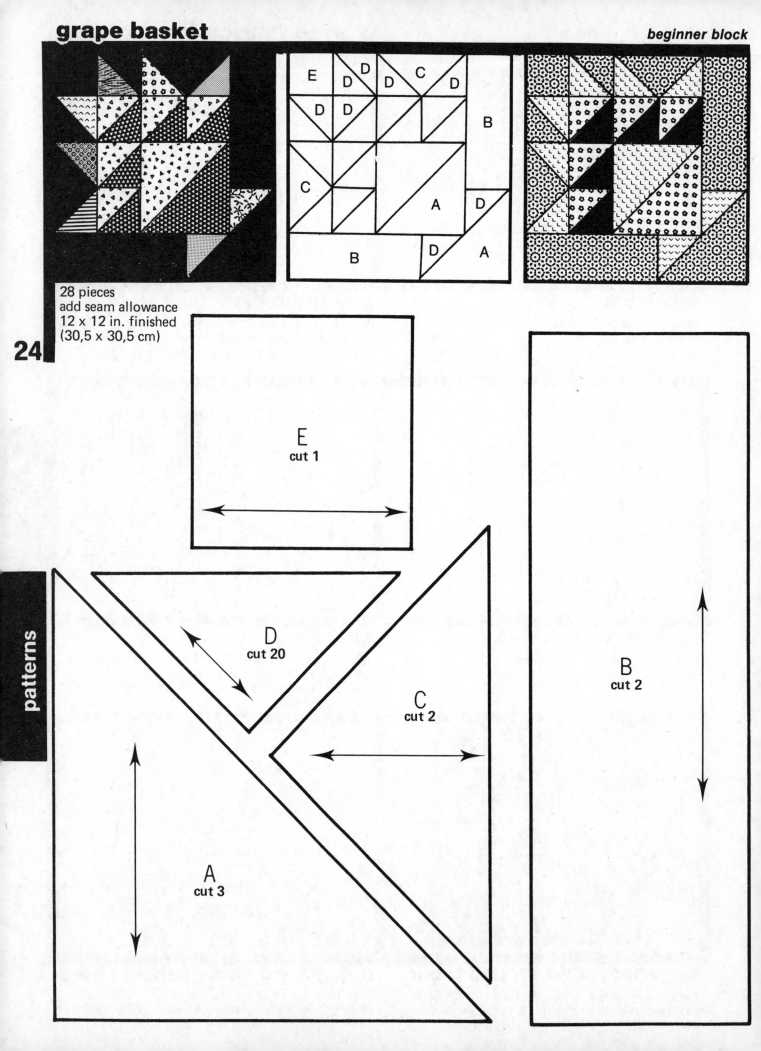

28 pieces
add seam allowance
12 x 12 in. finished
(30,5 x 30,5 cm)

24

patterns

E
cut 1

D
cut 20

C
cut 2

B
cut 2

A
cut 3

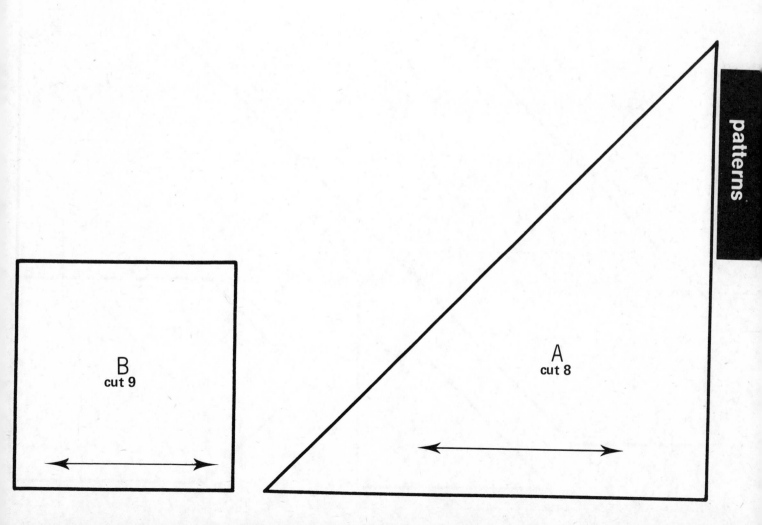

17 pieces
add seam allowance
12 x 12 in. finished
(30,5 x 30,5 cm)

25

patterns

B
cut 9

A
cut 8

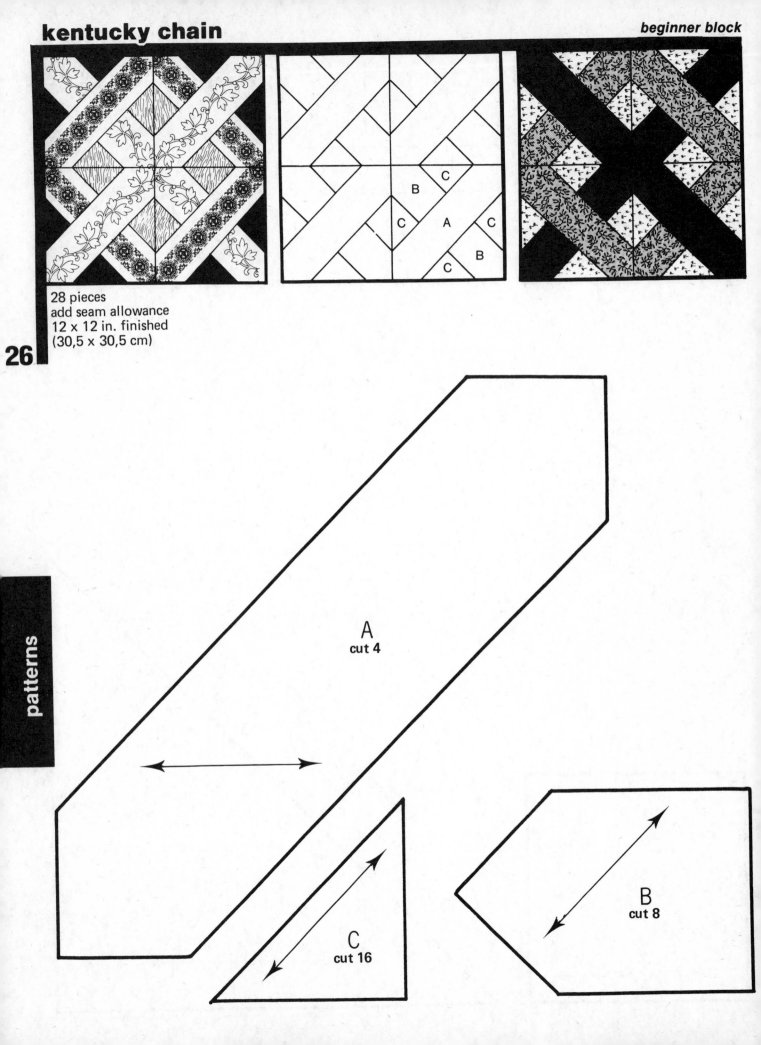

28 pieces
add seam allowance
12 x 12 in. finished
(30,5 x 30,5 cm)

26

patterns

A
cut 4

C
cut 16

B
cut 8

night and noon

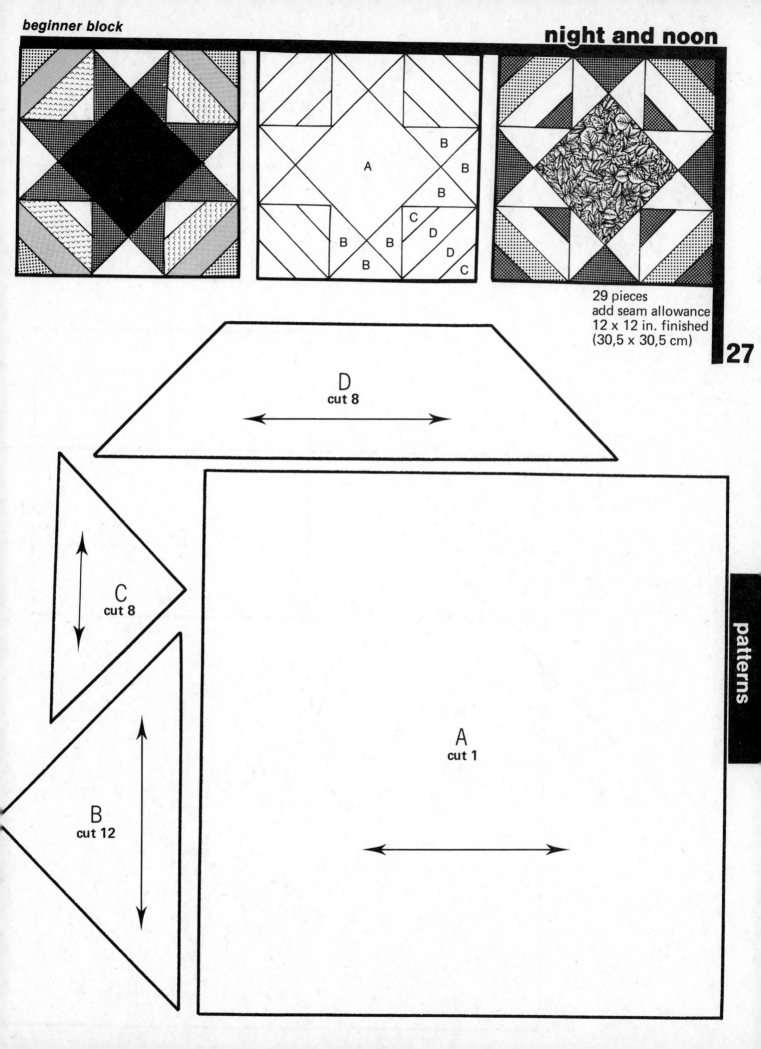

B
B
B
A
C
D
B
B
B
D
B
C

29 pieces
add seam allowance
12 x 12 in. finished
(30,5 x 30,5 cm)

D
cut 8

C
cut 8

B
cut 12

A
cut 1

patterns

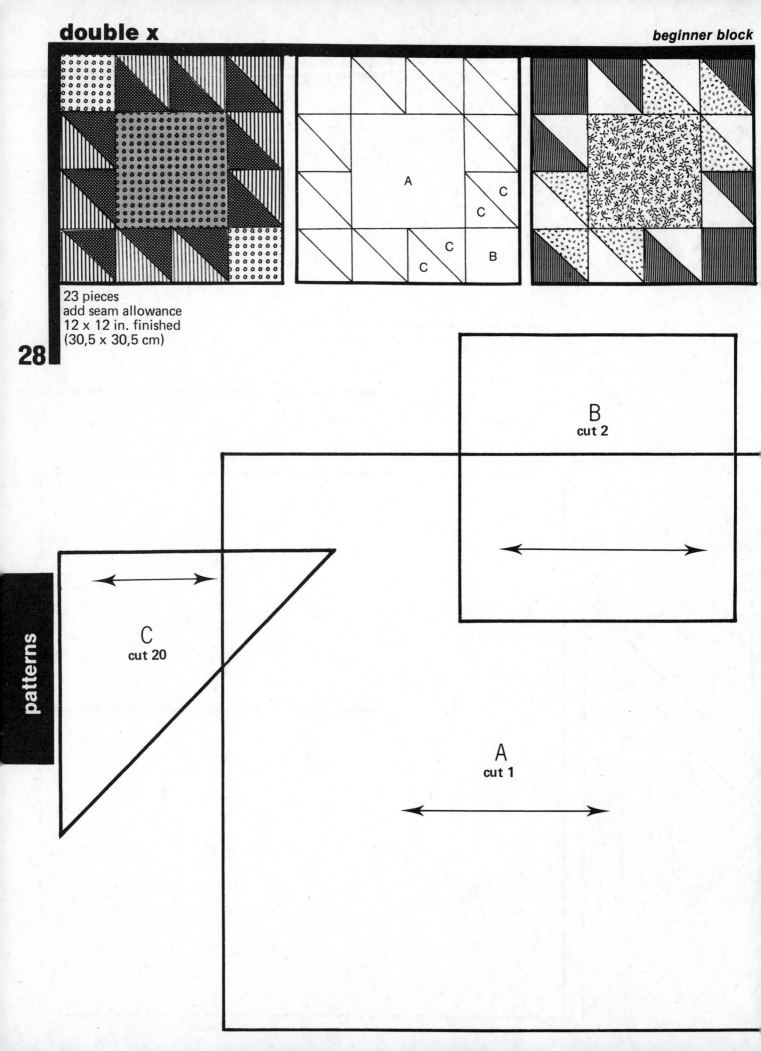

23 pieces
add seam allowance
12 x 12 in. finished
(30,5 x 30,5 cm)

28

A

C

C

C

C

B

B
cut 2

C
cut 20

A
cut 1

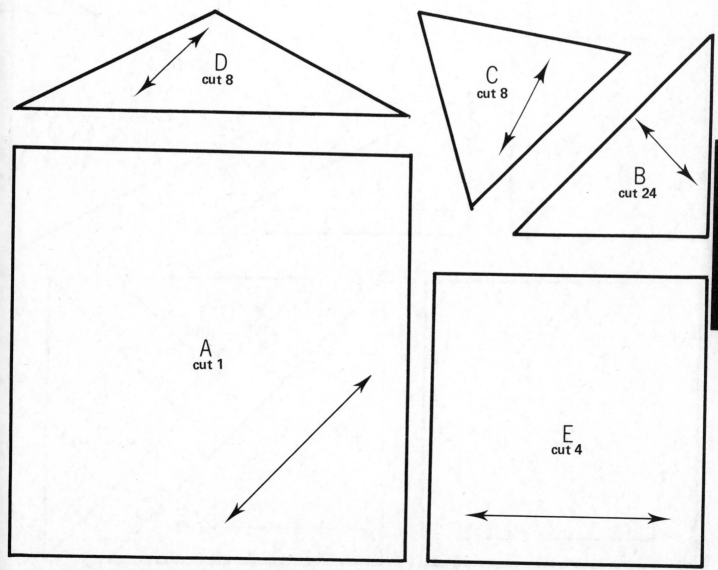

45 pieces
add seam allowance
12 x 12 in. finished
(30,5 x 30,5 cm)

D
cut 8

C
cut 8

B
cut 24

A
cut 1

E
cut 4

patterns

storm at sea

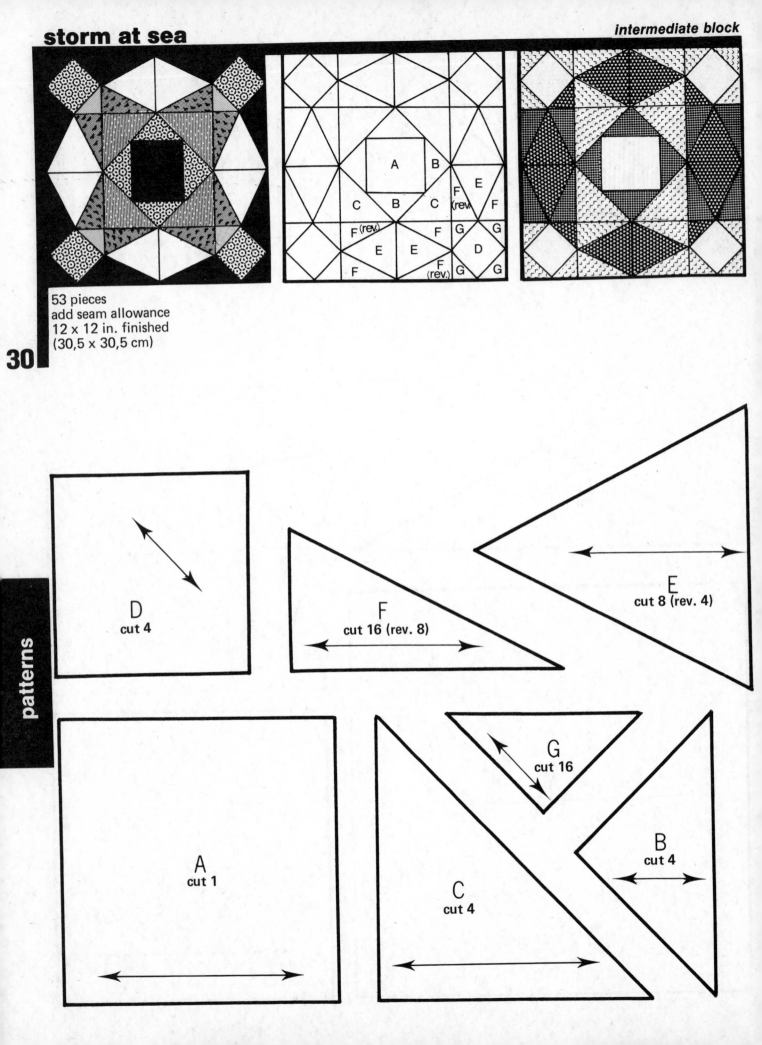

53 pieces
add seam allowance
12 x 12 in. finished
(30,5 x 30,5 cm)

30

patterns

D
cut 4

F
cut 16 (rev. 8)

E
cut 8 (rev. 4)

G
cut 16

B
cut 4

A
cut 1

C
cut 4

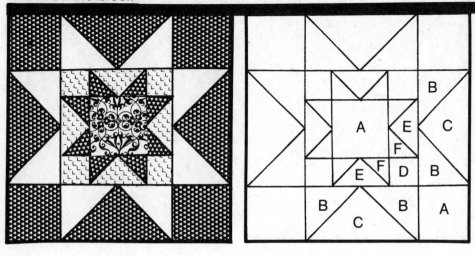

33 pieces
add seam allowance
12 x 12 in. finished
(30,5 x 30,5 cm)

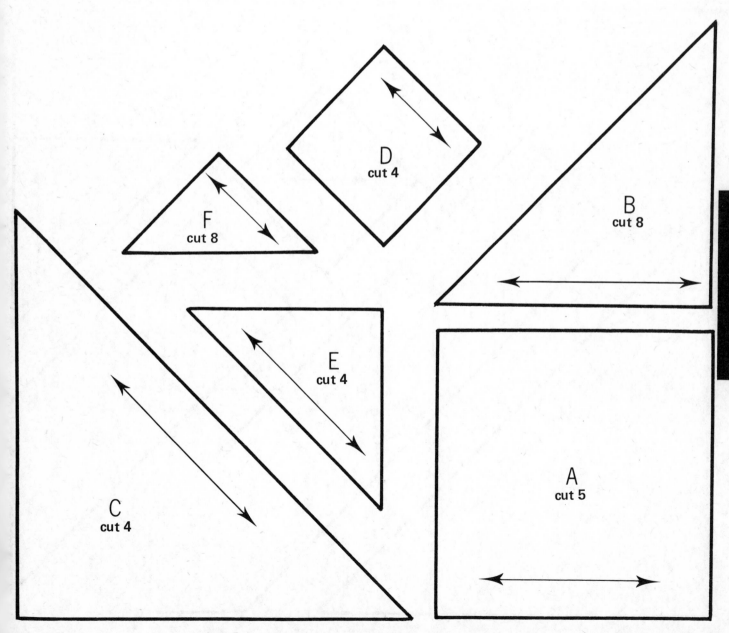

D
cut 4

F
cut 8

B
cut 8

E
cut 4

C
cut 4

A
cut 5

patterns

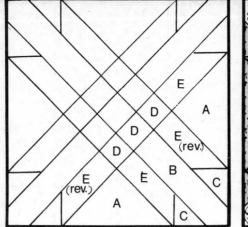

33 pieces
add seam allowance
12 x 12 in. finished
(30,5 x 30,5 cm)

32

patterns

D
cut 9

C
cut 8

B
cut 4

E
cut 8 (rev. 4)

A
cut 4

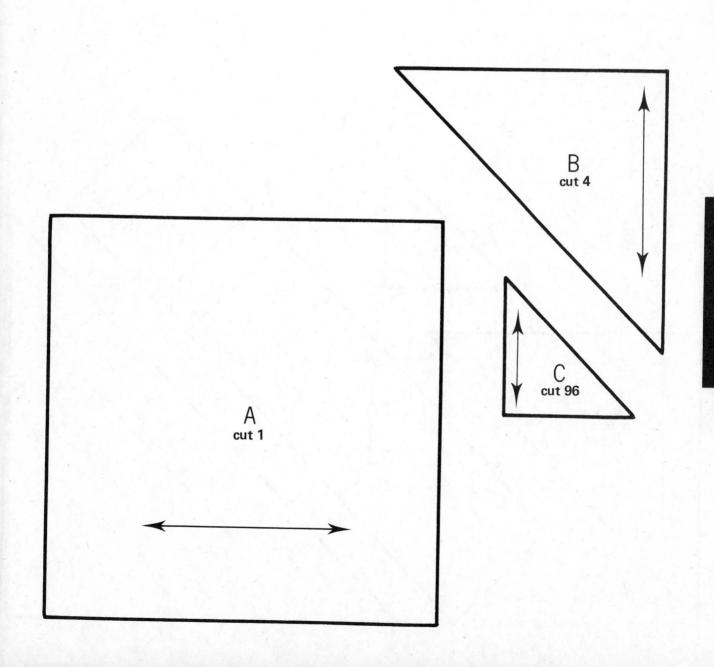

101 pieces
add seam allowance
12 x 12 in. finished
(30,5 x 30,5 cm)

33

B
cut 4

C
cut 96

patterns

A
cut 1

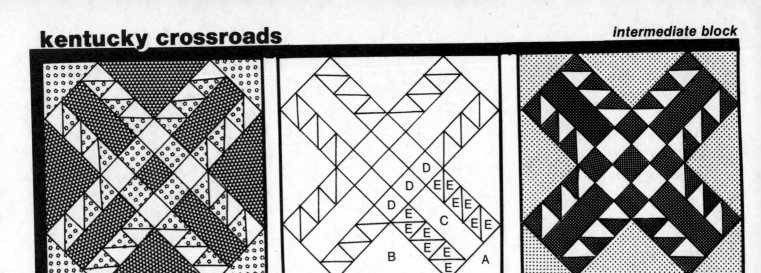

69 pieces
add seam allowance
12 x 12 in. finished
(30,5 x 30,5 cm)

34

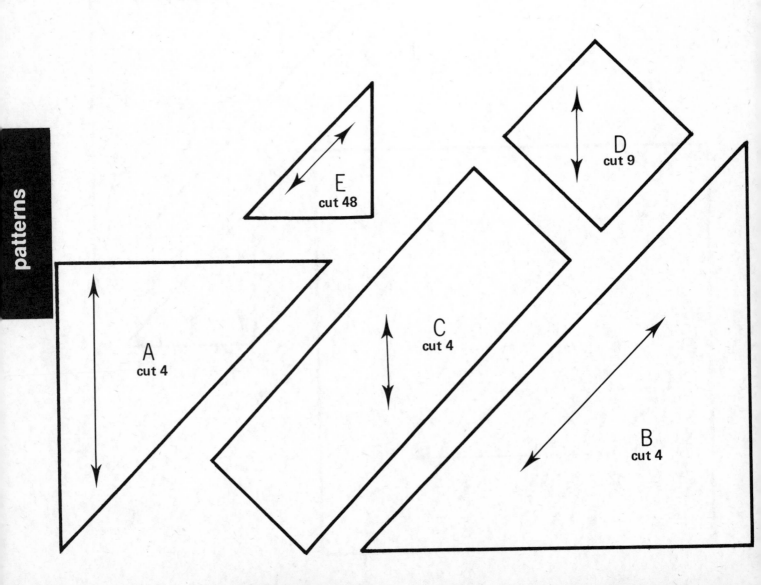

E cut 48

D cut 9

A cut 4

C cut 4

B cut 4

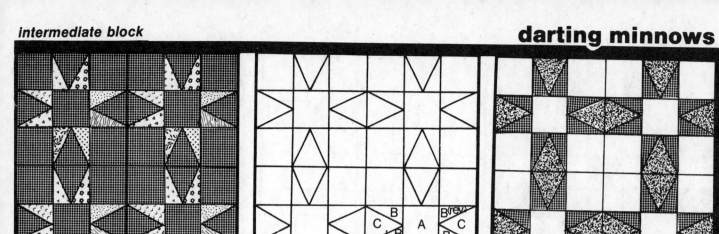

68 pieces
add seam allowance
12 x 12 in. finished
(30,5 x 30,5 cm)

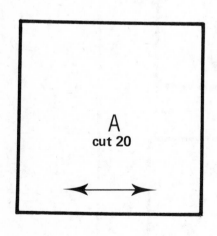

A
cut 20

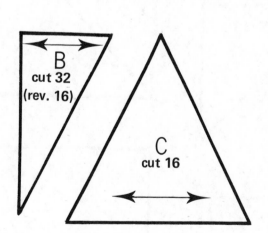

B
cut 32
(rev. 16)

C
cut 16

doe and darts

37 pieces
add seam allowance
12 x 12 in. finished
(30,5 x 30,5 cm)

36

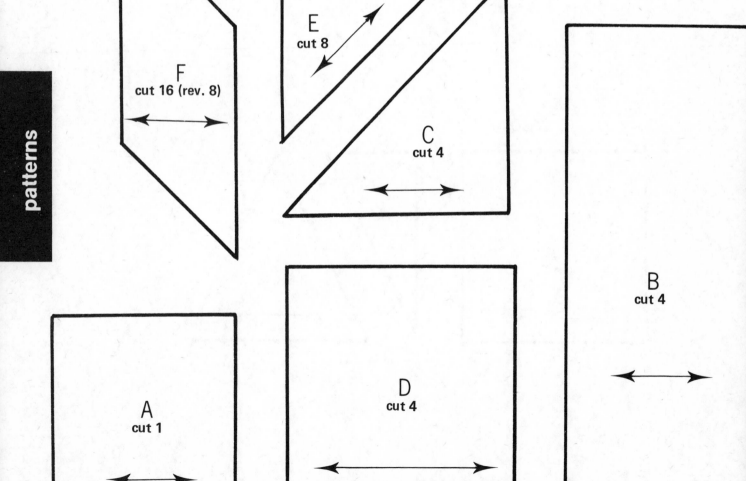

patterns

F
cut 16 (rev. 8)

E
cut 8

C
cut 4

B
cut 4

A
cut 1

D
cut 4

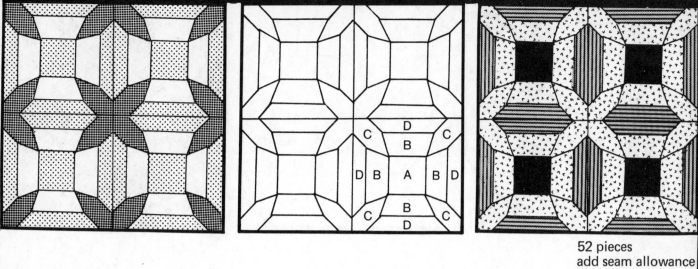

52 pieces
add seam allowance
12 x 12 in. finished
(30,5 x 30,5 cm)

patterns

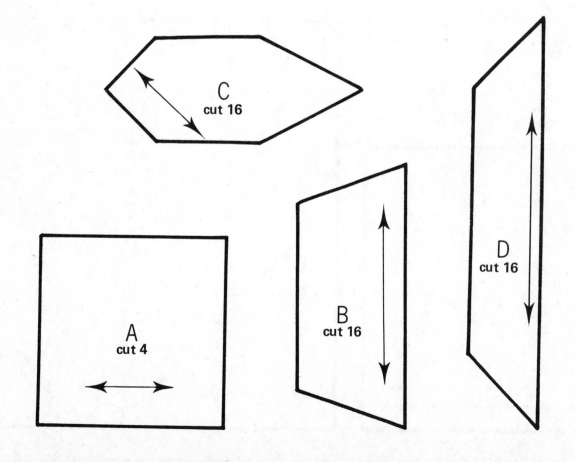

C
cut 16

D
cut 16

A
cut 4

B
cut 16

bachelor's puzzle

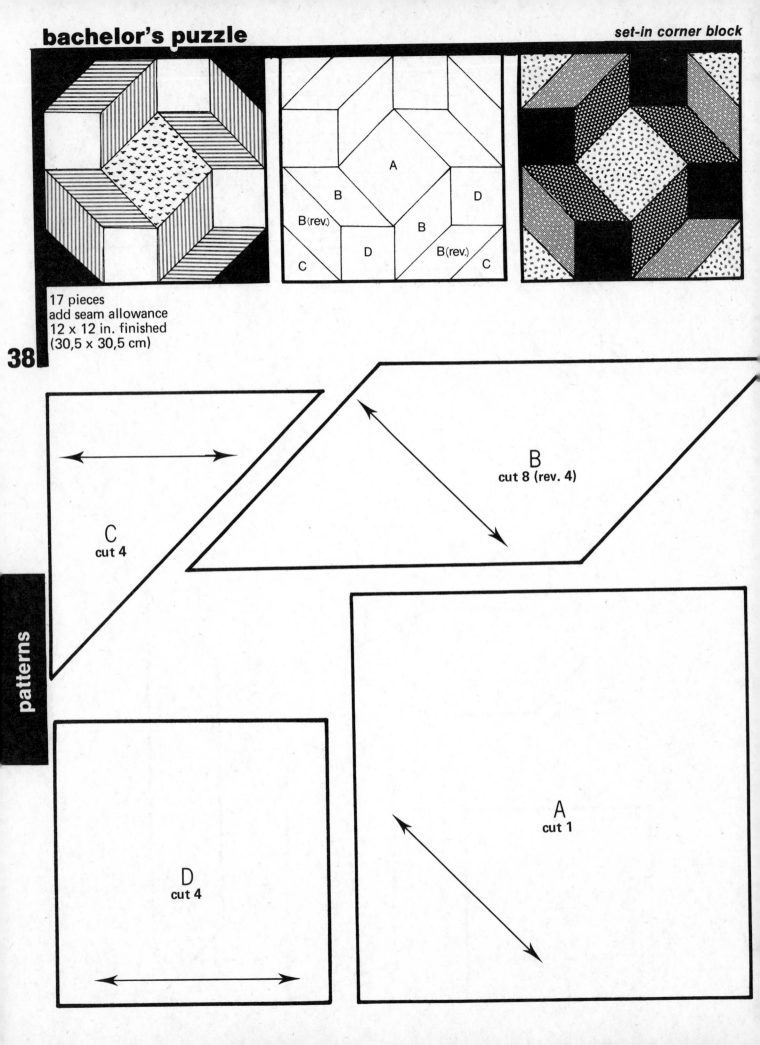

17 pieces
add seam allowance
12 x 12 in. finished
(30,5 x 30,5 cm)

38

A
B
B(rev.)
C
D
B
B(rev.)
D
C

patterns

C
cut 4

B
cut 8 (rev. 4)

D
cut 4

A
cut 1

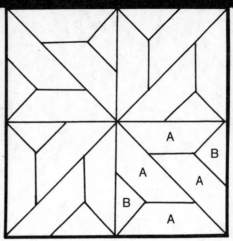

24 pieces
add seam allowance
12 x 12 in. finished
(30,5 x 30,5 cm)

39

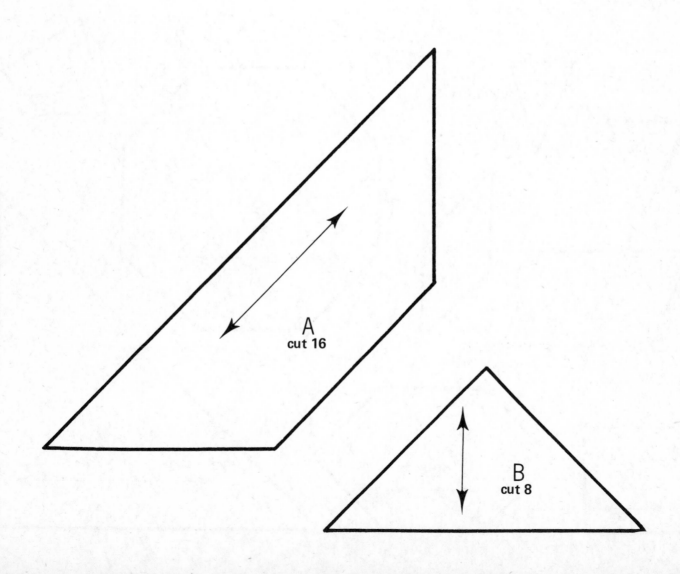

A
cut 16

B
cut 8

patterns

133 pieces
add seam allowance
12 x 12 in. finished
(30,5 x 30,5 cm)

40

patterns

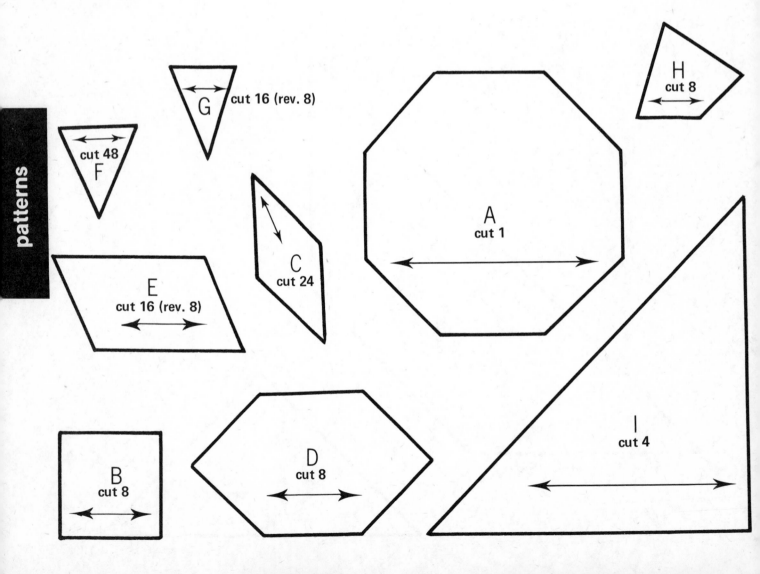

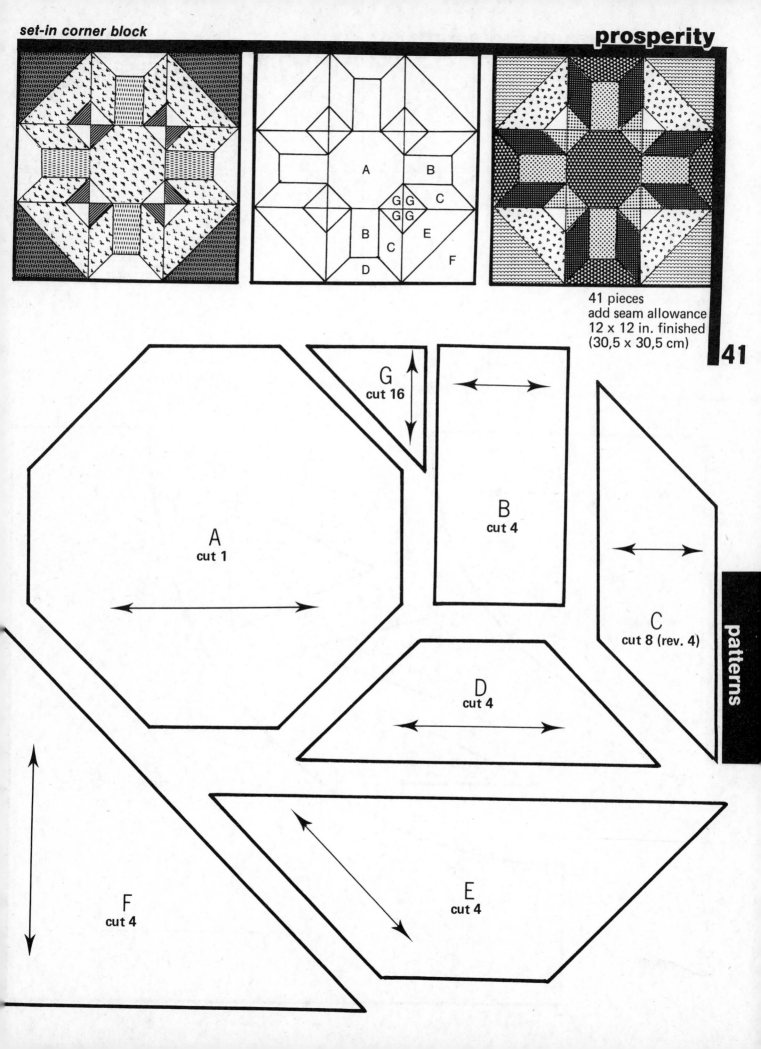

41 pieces
add seam allowance
12 x 12 in. finished
(30,5 x 30,5 cm)

41

G
cut 16

B
cut 4

A
cut 1

C
cut 8 (rev. 4)

patterns

D
cut 4

F
cut 4

E
cut 4

sawtooth drunkard's path

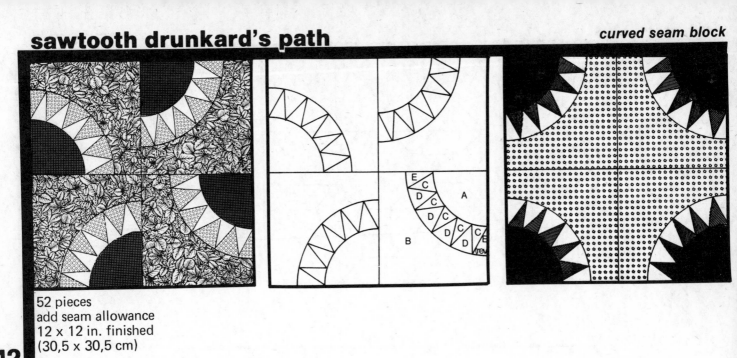

52 pieces
add seam allowance
12 x 12 in. finished
(30,5 x 30,5 cm)

42

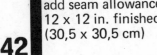

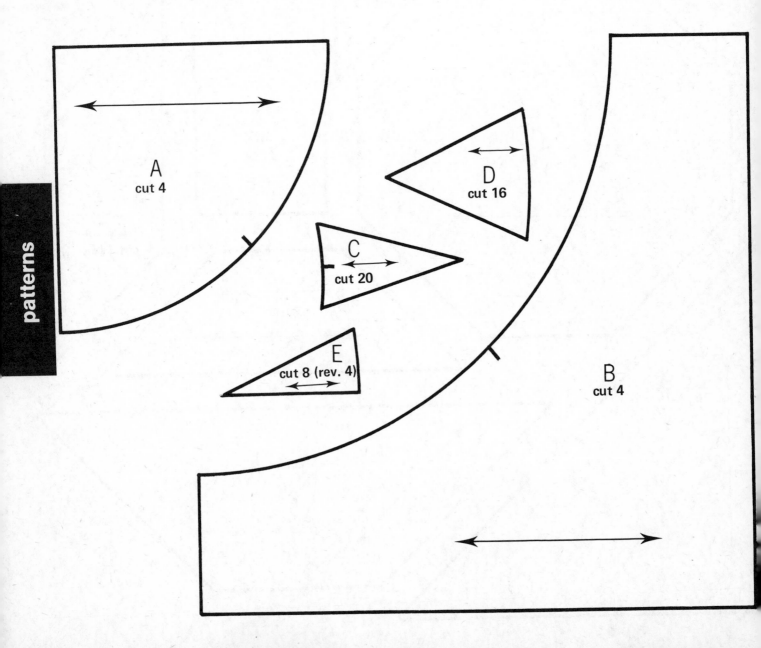

A
cut 4

D
cut 16

C
cut 20

E
cut 8 (rev. 4)

B
cut 4

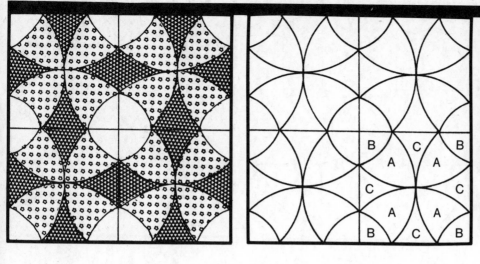

48 pieces
add seam allowance
12 x 12 in. finished
(30,5 x 30,5 cm)

43

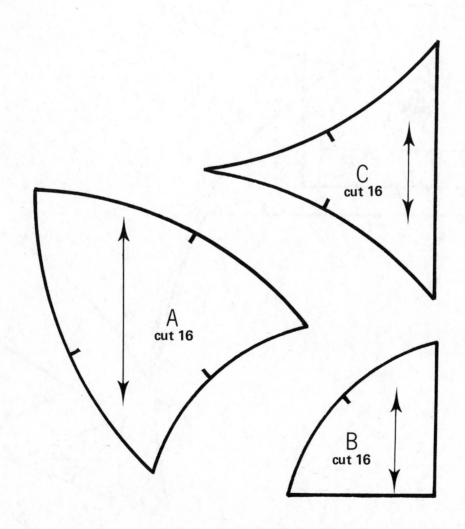

C
cut 16

A
cut 16

B
cut 16

patterns

oriole window

curved seam block

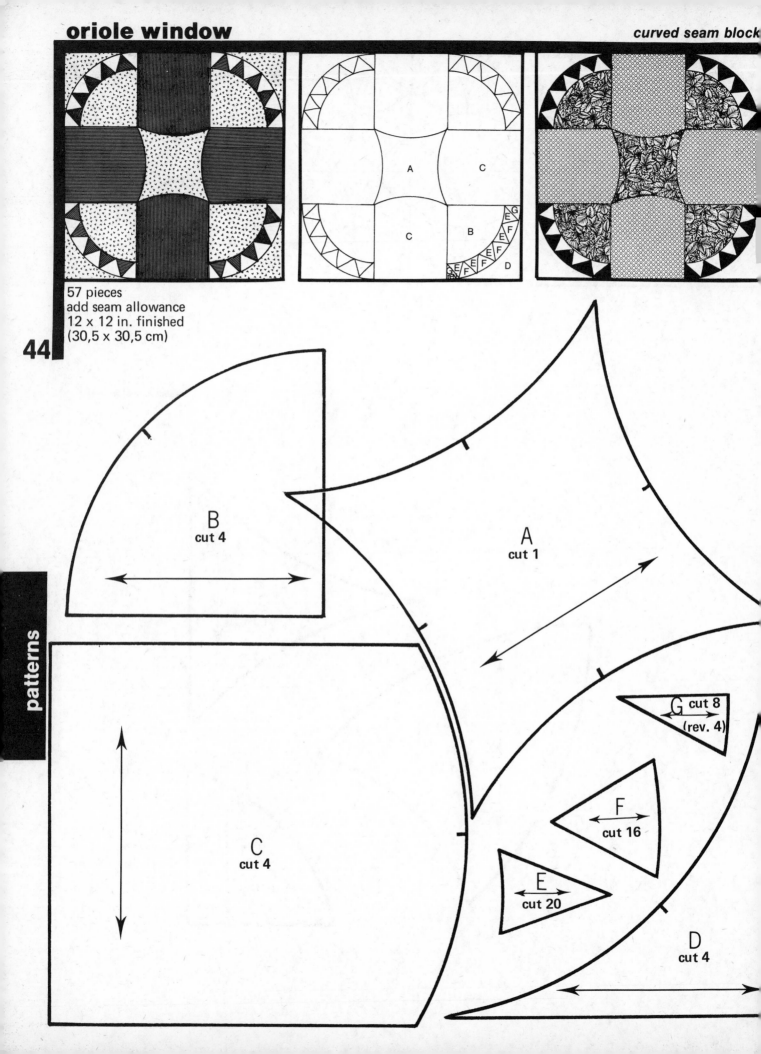

57 pieces
add seam allowance
12 x 12 in. finished
(30,5 x 30,5 cm)

44

patterns

B
cut 4

A
cut 1

G cut 8
(rev. 4)

F
cut 16

C
cut 4

E
cut 20

D
cut 4

sampler quilt by **Lisa Taylor**

wall quilt by
Terry Hedani

wall quilt by **Barbara Eidlhuber**

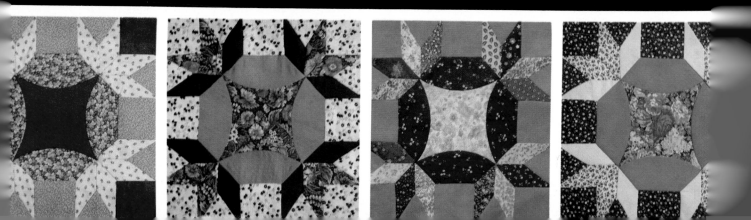

sampler quilt by **Lynn Connell**

sampler quilt *by* **Mary Lee Winterkorn**

sampler quilt by **Lynn McBratney**

sampler quilt by **Roxanna Sue**

double wedding ring

A
B
C
C (rev.)
D
D (rev.)
E

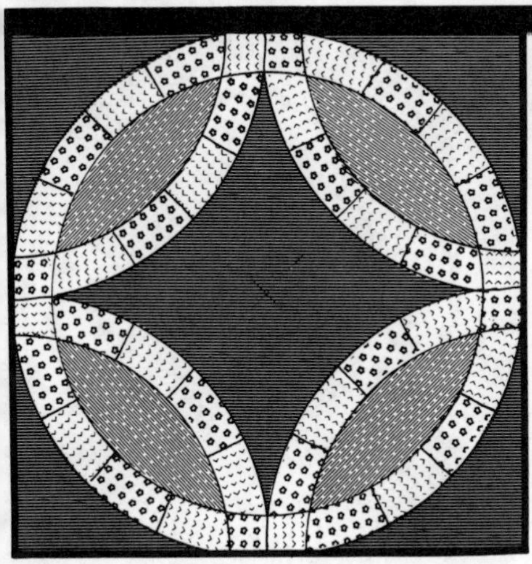

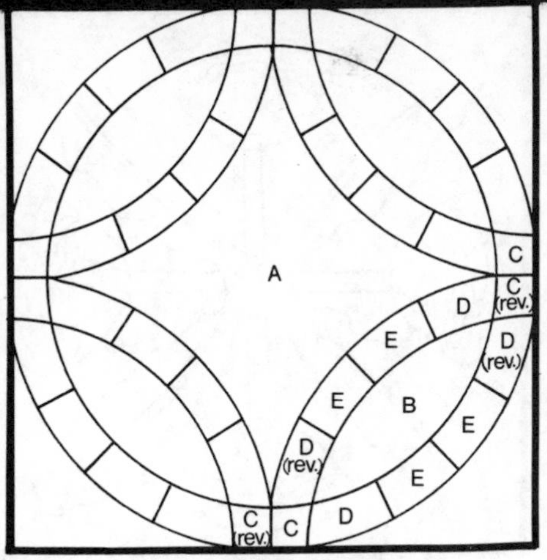

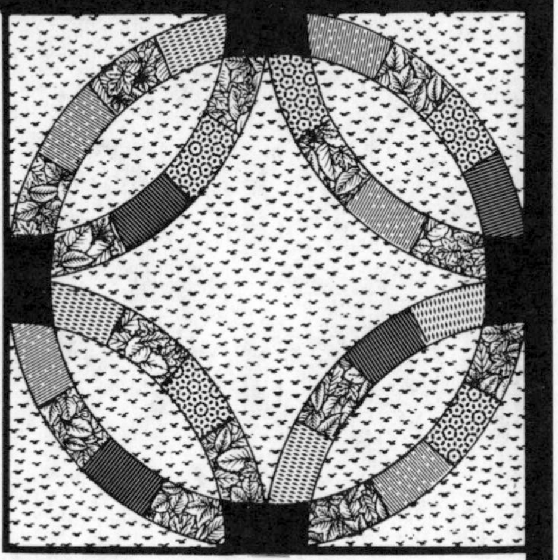

49 pieces
add seam allowance
12 x 12 in. finished (30,5 x 30,5 cm)

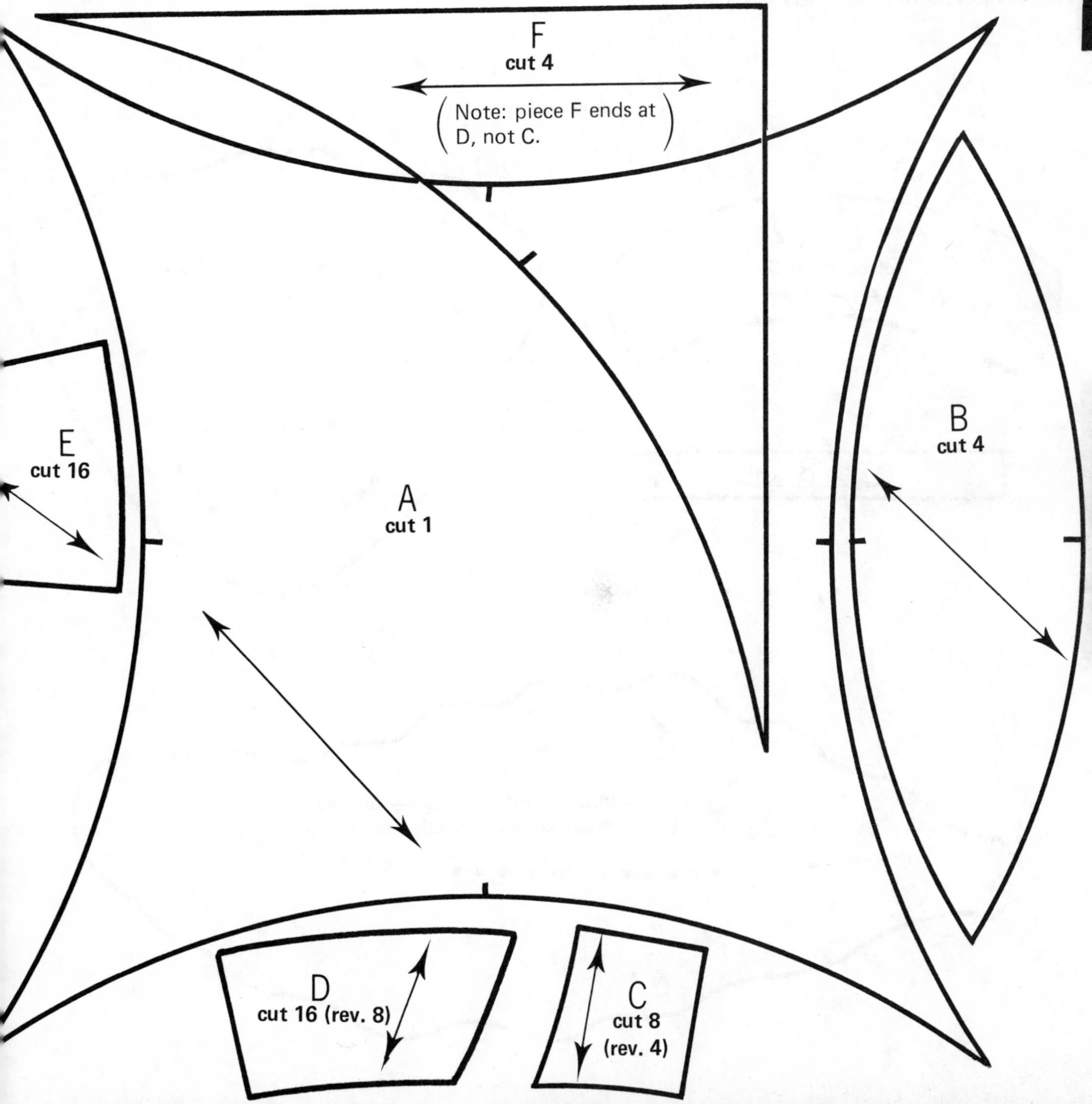

F
cut 4
Note: piece F ends at D, not C.
E
cut 16
A
cut 1
B
cut 4
D
cut 16 (rev. 8)
C
cut 8
(rev. 4)

currents and coxcombs

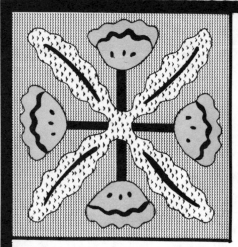 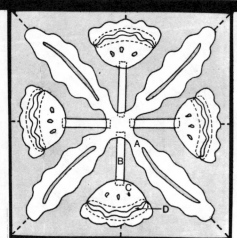 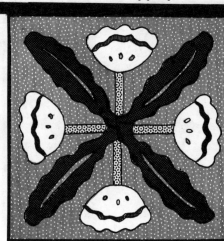

13 pieces
see page 21 for seam allowance
cut background 13 x 13 in. (33 x 33 cm)

54

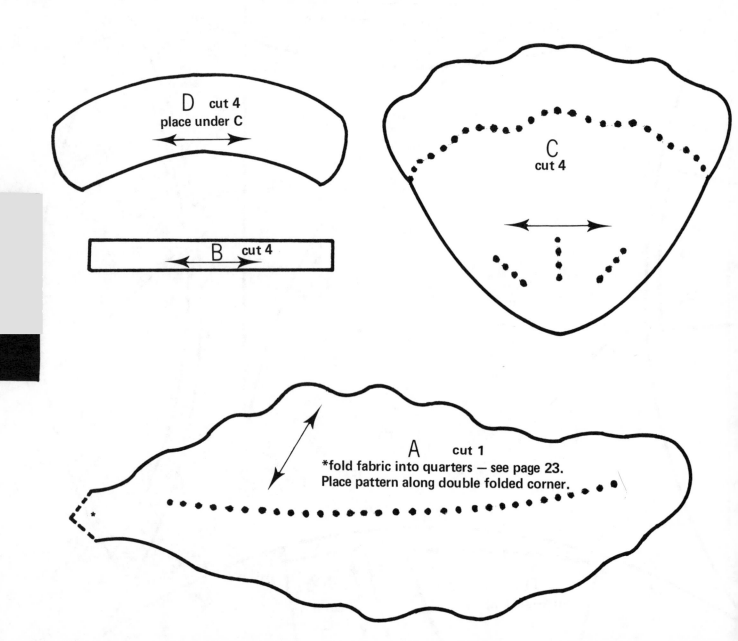

D cut 4
place under C

B cut 4

C
cut 4

A cut 1
*fold fabric into quarters — see page 23.
Place pattern along double folded corner.

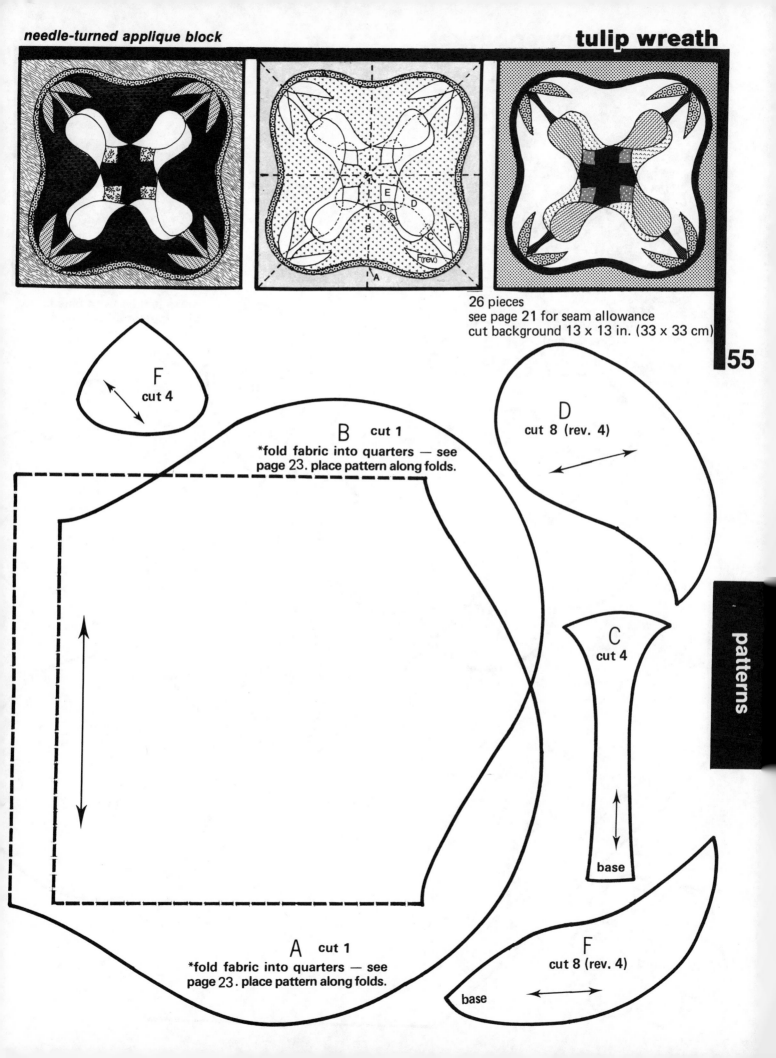

26 pieces
see page 21 for seam allowance
cut background 13 x 13 in. (33 x 33 cm)

F
cut 4

B cut 1
*fold fabric into quarters — see
page 23. place pattern along folds.

D
cut 8 (rev. 4)

C
cut 4

base

patterns

A cut 1
*fold fabric into quarters — see
page 23. place pattern along folds.

F
cut 8 (rev. 4)

base

appliqued flower basket

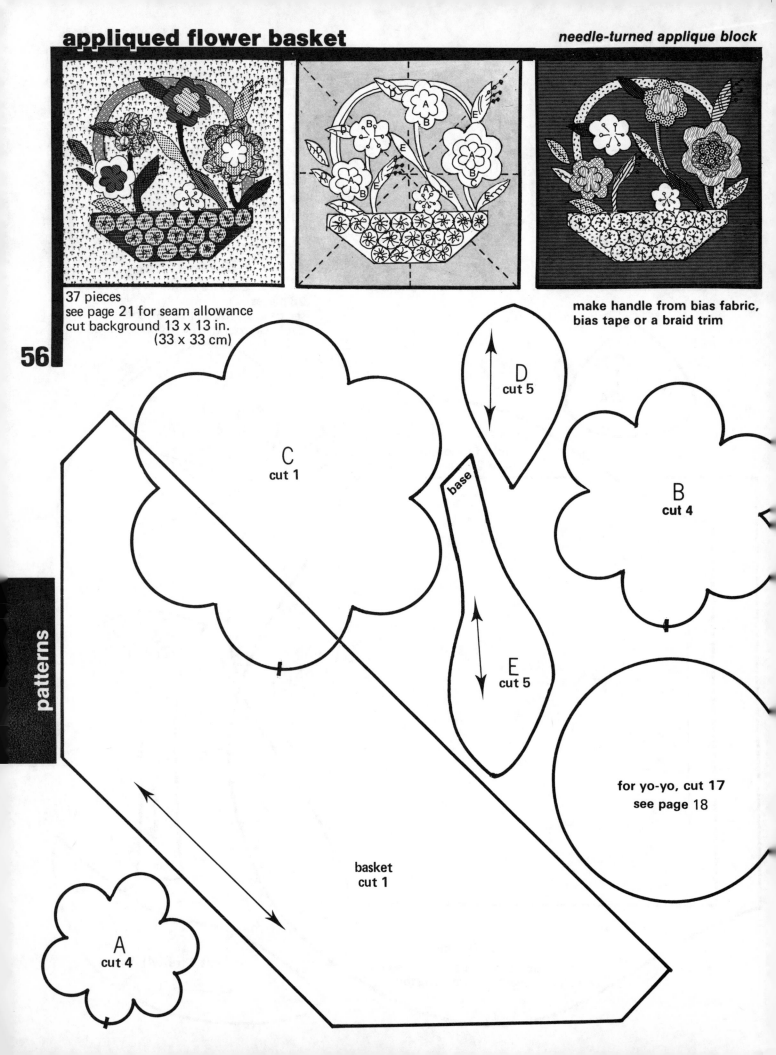

37 pieces
see page 21 for seam allowance
cut background 13 x 13 in.
(33 x 33 cm)

56

make handle from bias fabric,
bias tape or a braid trim

D
cut 5

C
cut 1

base

B
cut 4

patterns

E
cut 5

for yo-yo, cut 17
see page 18

basket
cut 1

A
cut 4

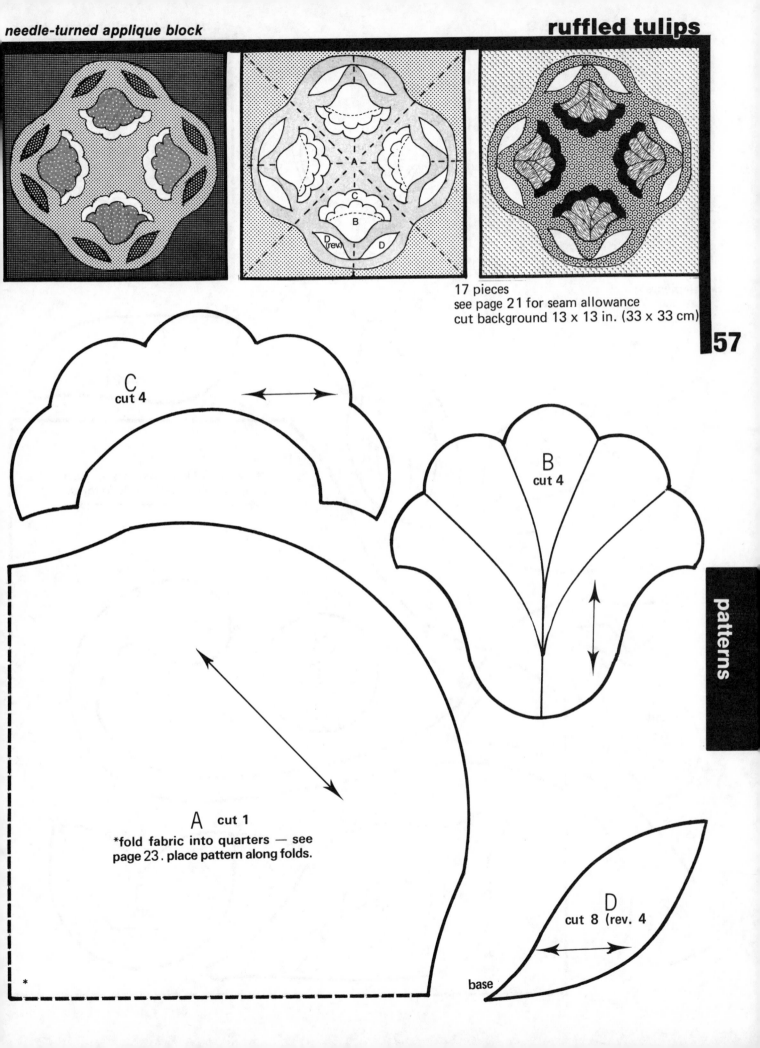

17 pieces
see page 21 for seam allowance
cut background 13 x 13 in. (33 x 33 cm)

57

C cut 4

B cut 4

patterns

A cut 1
*fold fabric into quarters — see
page 23. place pattern along folds.

D cut 8 (rev. 4

base

el modena rose

14 pieces
see page 21 for seam allowance
cut background 13 x 13 in. (33 x 33 cm)

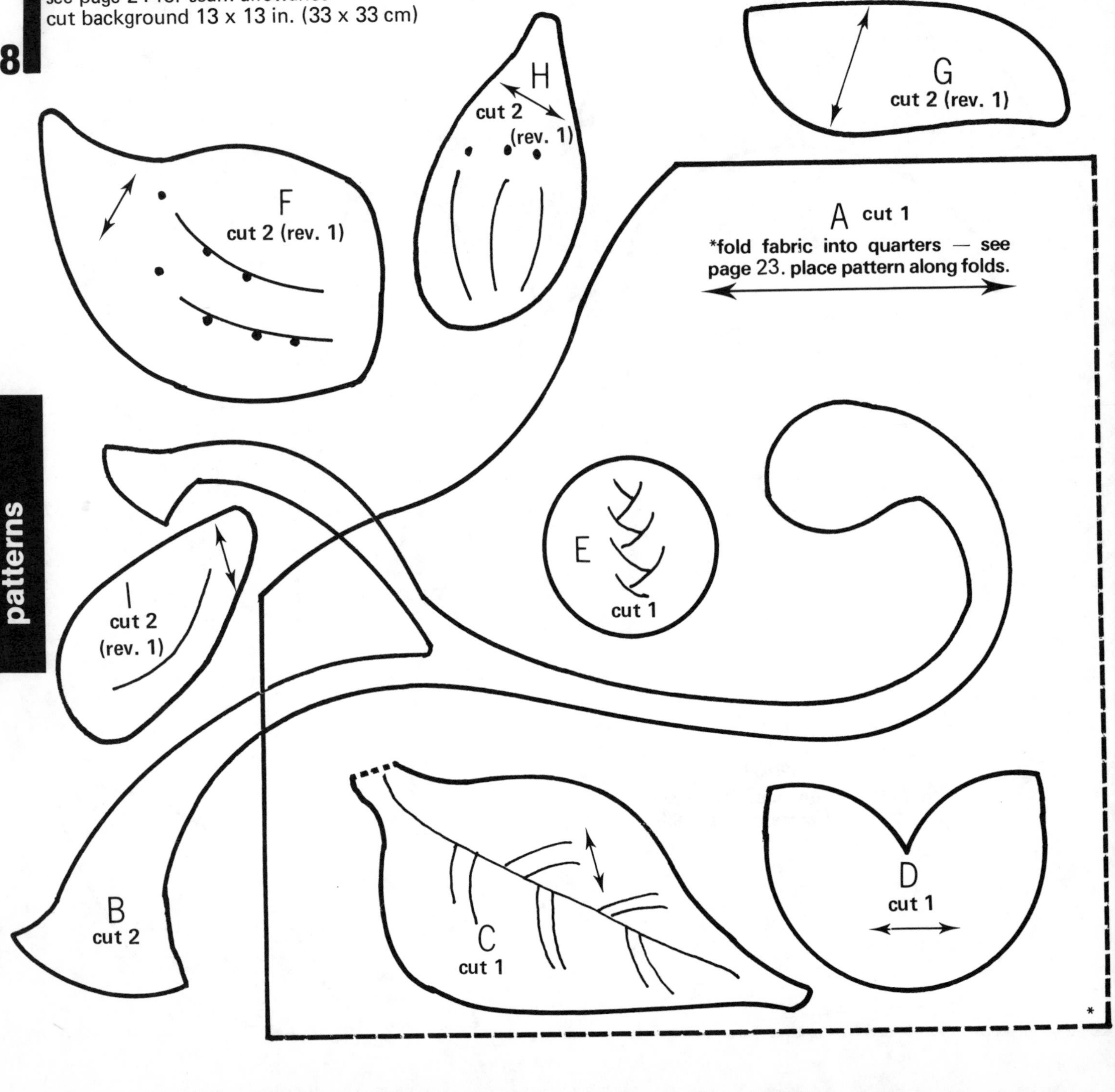

58

patterns

H
cut 2
(rev. 1)

G
cut 2 (rev. 1)

F
cut 2 (rev. 1)

A cut 1
*fold fabric into quarters — see
page 23. place pattern along folds.

E
cut 1

I
cut 2
(rev. 1)

B
cut 2

C
cut 1

D
cut 1

*

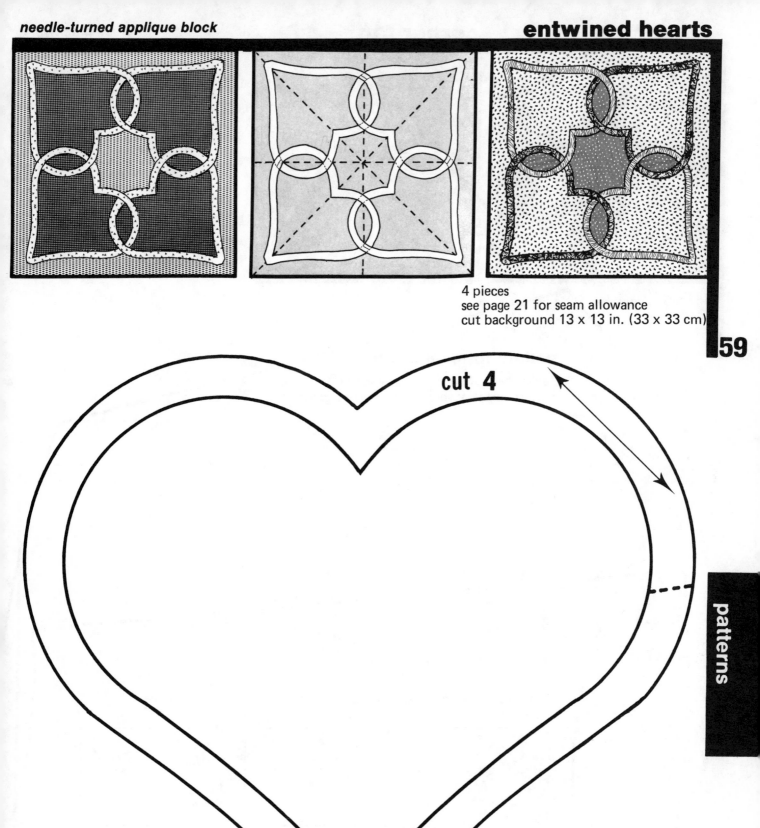

4 pieces
see page 21 for seam allowance
cut background 13 x 13 in. (33 x 33 cm)

cut **4**

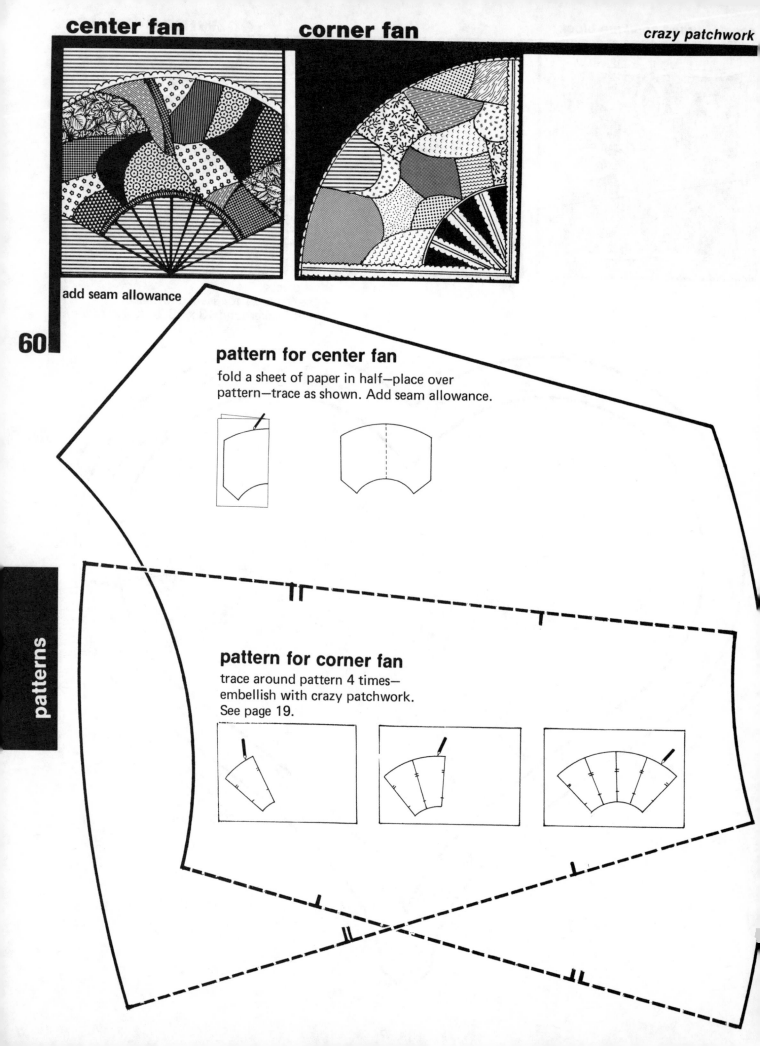

add seam allowance

pattern for center fan

fold a sheet of paper in half—place over
pattern—trace as shown. Add seam allowance.

pattern for corner fan

trace around pattern 4 times—
embellish with crazy patchwork.
See page 19.

60 pieces
add seam allowance
12 x 12 in. finished
(30,5 x 30,5 cm)

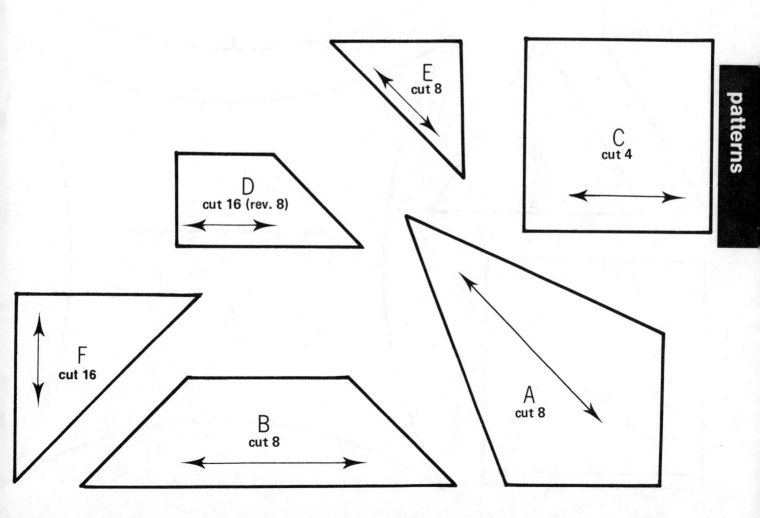

E
cut 8

C
cut 4

D
cut 16 (rev. 8)

F
cut 16

B
cut 8

A
cut 8

patterns

hands all around

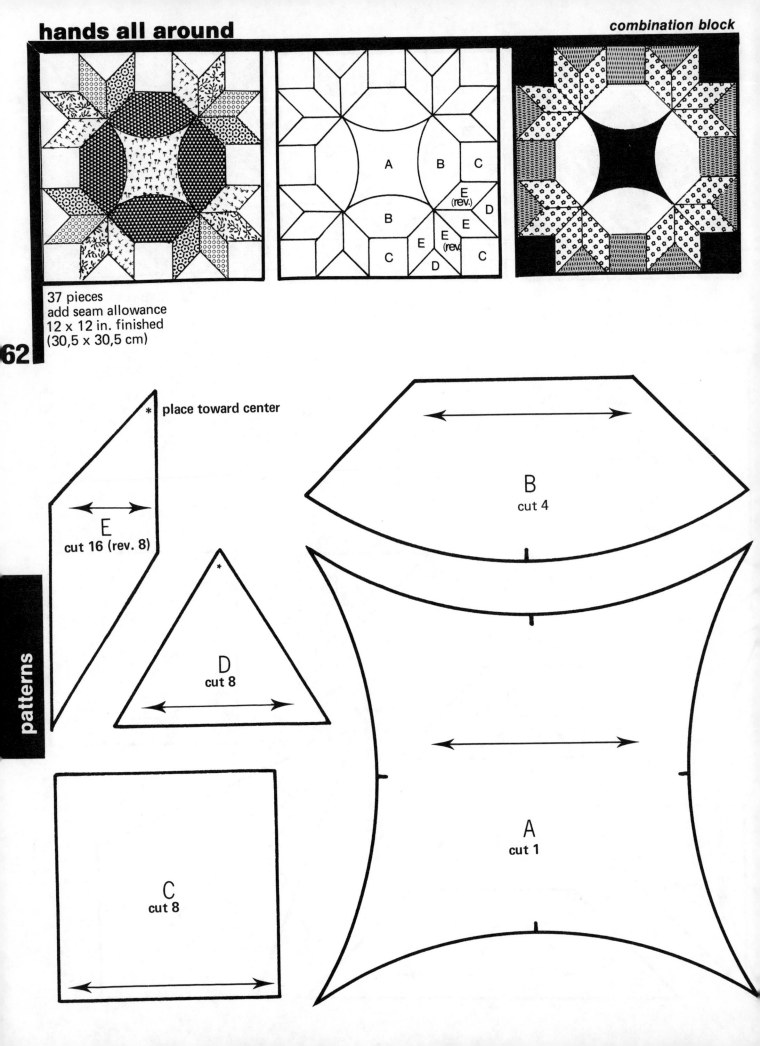

37 pieces
add seam allowance
12 x 12 in. finished
(30,5 x 30,5 cm)

62

patterns

* place toward center

E
cut 16 (rev. 8)

B
cut 4

D
cut 8

C
cut 8

A
cut 1

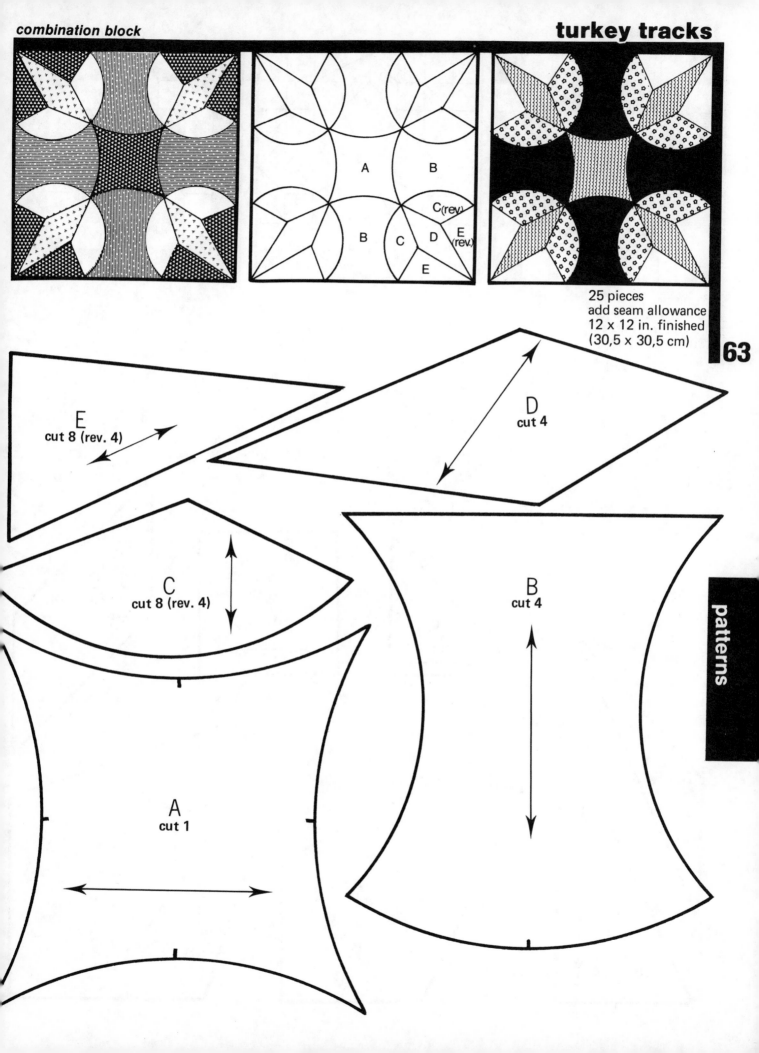

A B

C (rev.)

B C D E (rev.)

E

25 pieces
add seam allowance
12 x 12 in. finished
(30,5 x 30,5 cm)

63

E
cut 8 (rev. 4)

D
cut 4

C
cut 8 (rev. 4)

B
cut 4

A
cut 1

patterns

little giant

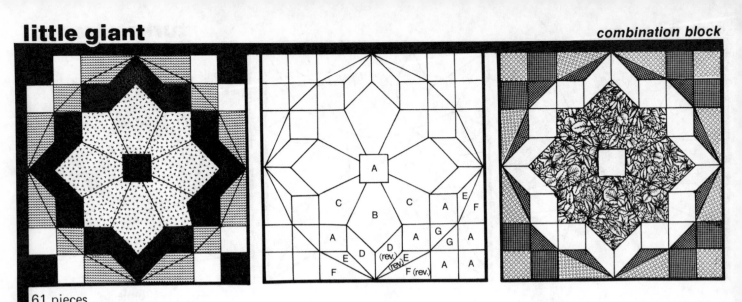

61 pieces
add seam allowance
12 x 12 in. finished
(30,5 x 30,5 cm)

64

patterns

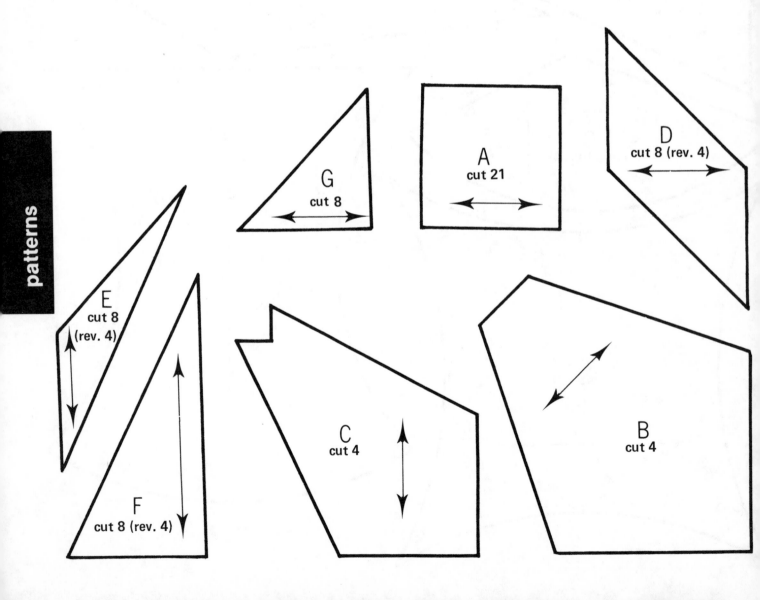

G
cut 8

A
cut 21

D
cut 8 (rev. 4)

E
cut 8
(rev. 4)

F
cut 8 (rev. 4)

C
cut 4

B
cut 4

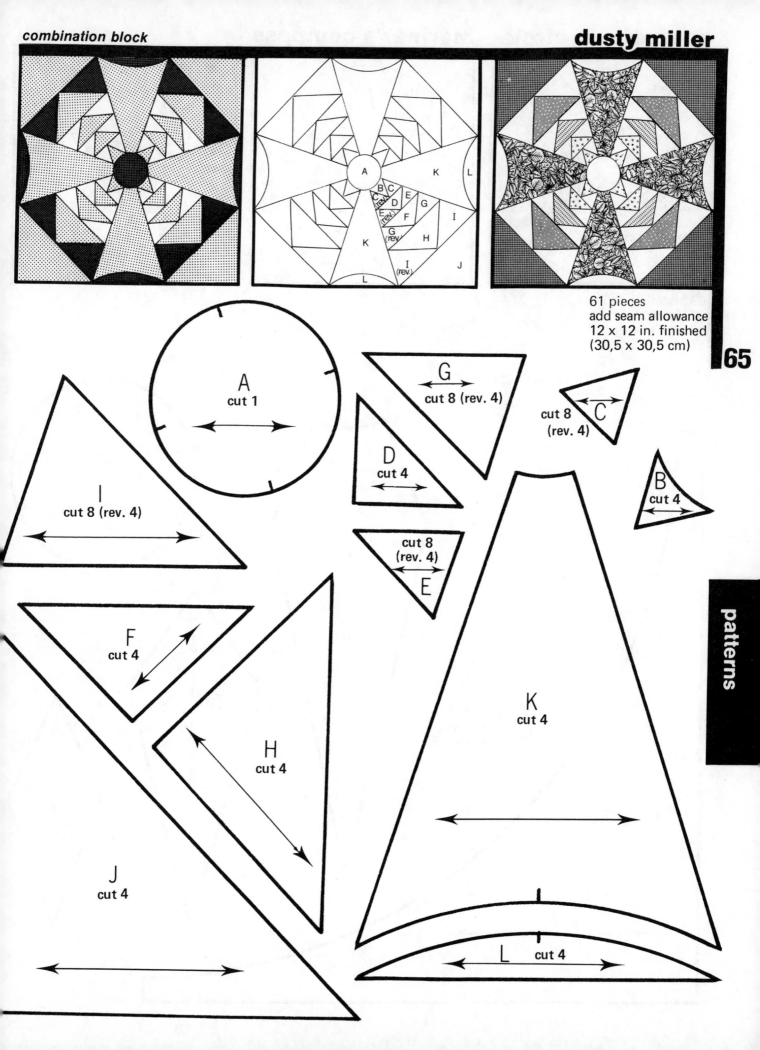

61 pieces
add seam allowance
12 x 12 in. finished
(30,5 x 30,5 cm)

65

A
cut 1

G
cut 8 (rev. 4)

cut 8
(rev. 4)
C

D
cut 4

B
cut 4

I
cut 8 (rev. 4)

cut 8
(rev. 4)
E

F
cut 4

patterns

K
cut 4

H
cut 4

J
cut 4

L   cut 4

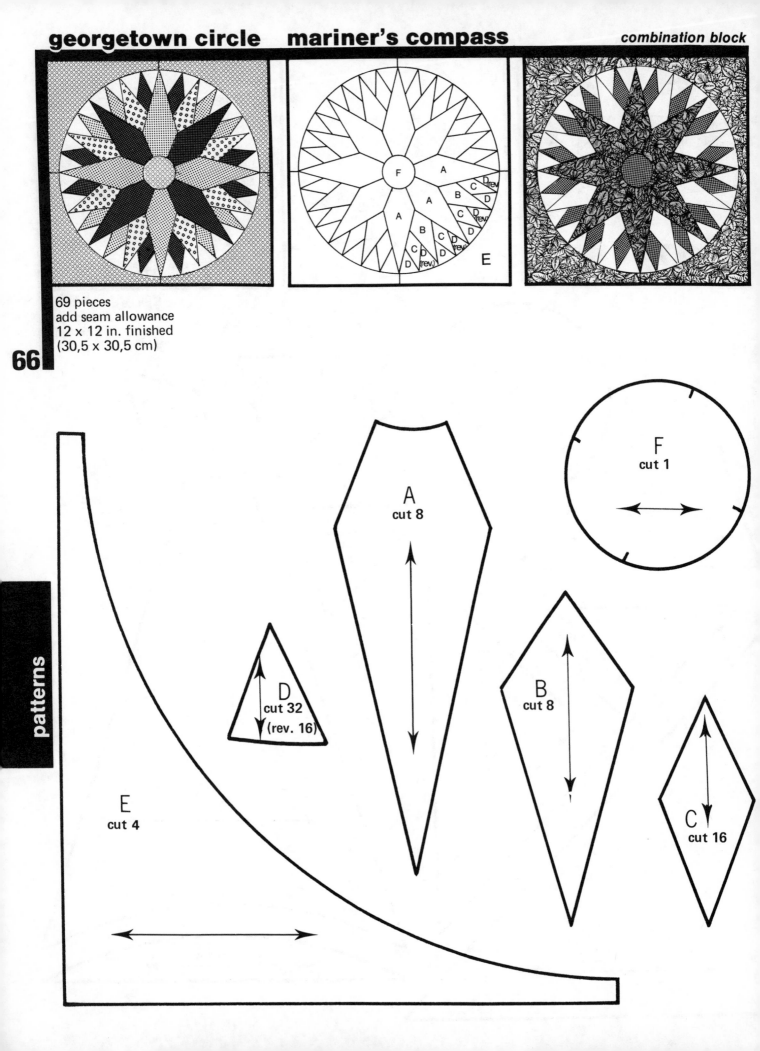

69 pieces
add seam allowance
12 x 12 in. finished
(30,5 x 30,5 cm)

66

F
cut 1

A
cut 8

D
cut 32
(rev. 16)

B
cut 8

C
cut 16

E
cut 4

patterns

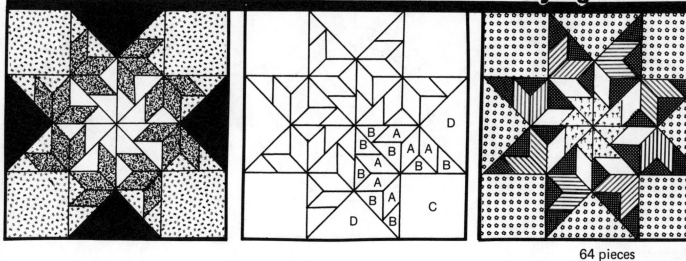

64 pieces
add seam allowance
12 x 12 in. finished
(30,5 x 30,5 cm)

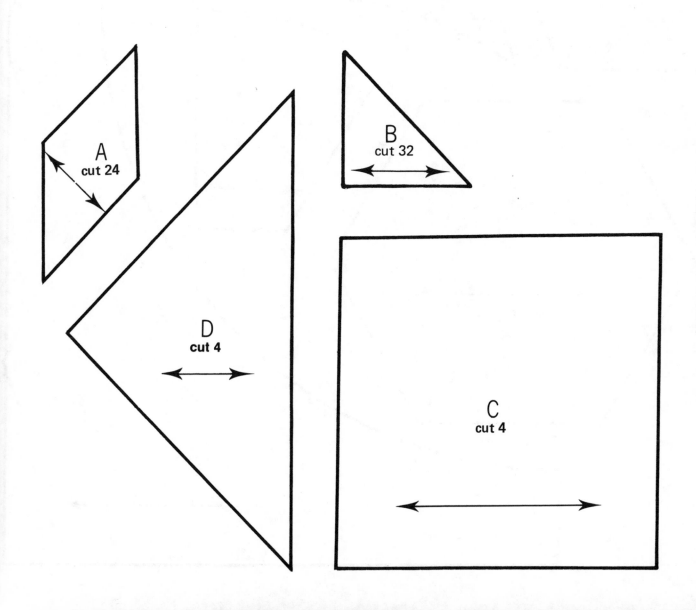

A
cut 24

B
cut 32

D
cut 4

C
cut 4

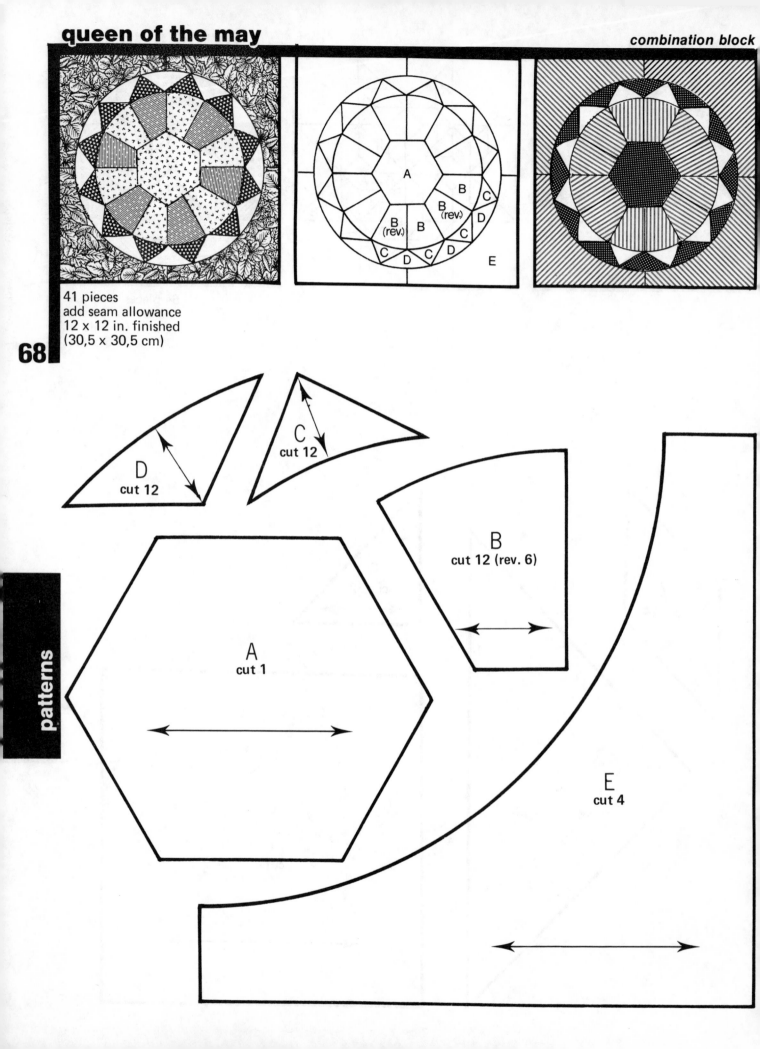

41 pieces
add seam allowance
12 x 12 in. finished
(30,5 x 30,5 cm)

68

A
cut 1

B
cut 12 (rev. 6)

C
cut 12

D
cut 12

E
cut 4

patterns

48 pieces
add seam allowance
12 x 12 in. finished
(30,5 x 30,5 cm)

69

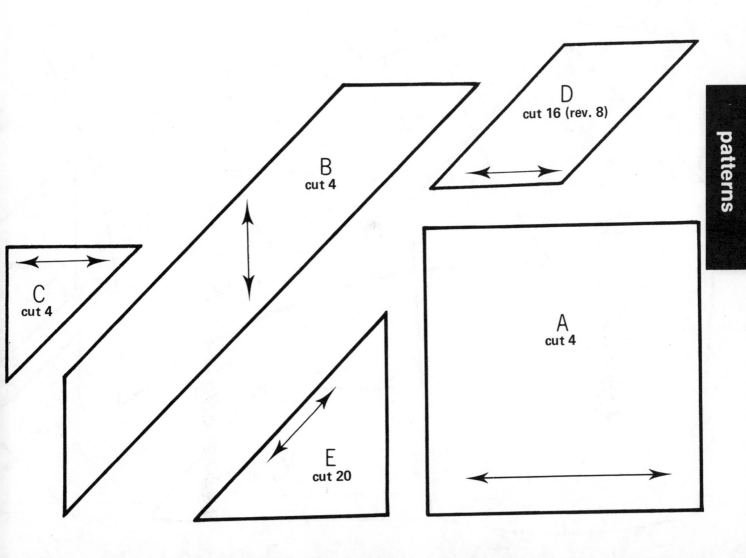

B
cut 4

D
cut 16 (rev. 8)

patterns

C
cut 4

A
cut 4

E
cut 20

friendship knot

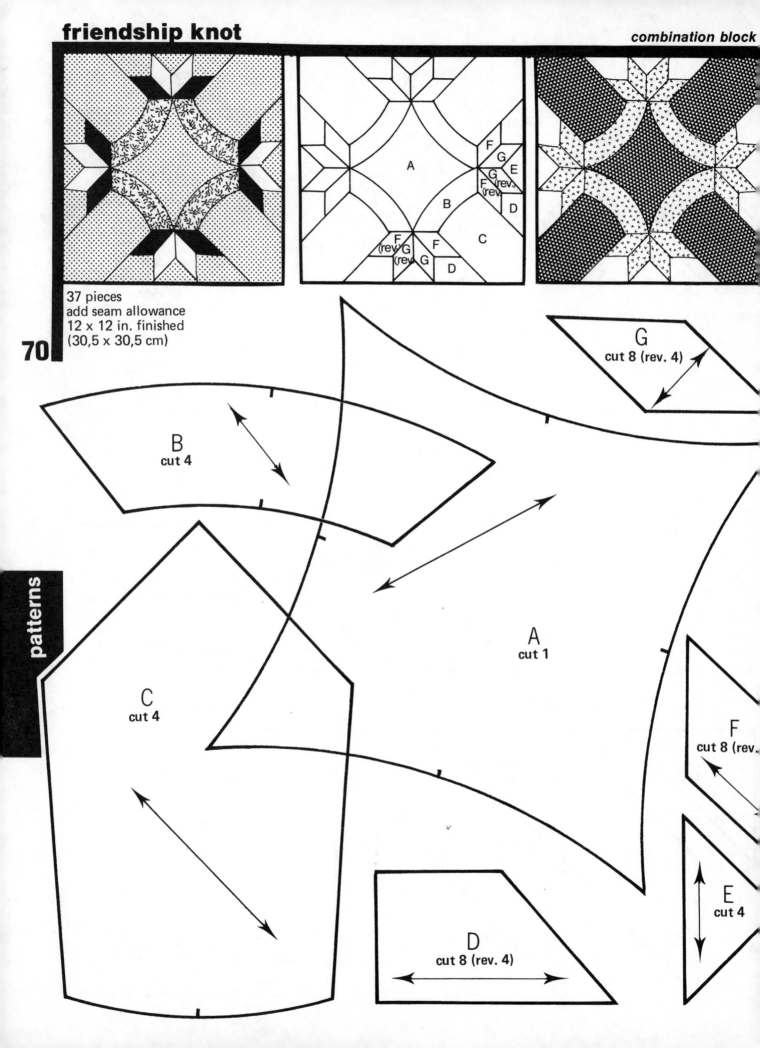

37 pieces
add seam allowance
12 x 12 in. finished
(30,5 x 30,5 cm)

70

patterns

G
cut 8 (rev. 4)

B
cut 4

A
cut 1

C
cut 4

F
cut 8 (rev.

E
cut 4

D
cut 8 (rev. 4)

good balance

poor balance

patterns

Most of the quilts shown in this book have been designed combining six to nine blocks. You can use more blocks to make a larger top but the final design will still need balancing.

When I finish a block, I immediately square it so I won't continue to stitch blocks larger or smaller than 12½ in. (31,8cm) (including seam allowance). Sometimes a block will be lopsided, have irregular edges, or pucker. You may have to re-make the block or re-sew a few seams. All the patterns in this book are for 12 in. (30,5cm) blocks but will measure 12½ in. square (31,8cm) because of the unsewn outside seam allowance. If a block measures just a little larger, it can be eased along its seam. A block that is smaller, however, is useless and will need to be brought up to size.

Check a block's size by placing a 12 in. square (30,5cm) sandpaper template over its wrong side. The ¼-in. (6mm) seam allowance should be showing along all four edges. Re-sew until the block is square and correct in size. Mark the outside seam allowance using a sharp pencil.

The blocks within a sampler quilt can be arranged in a number of ways. You will need to work with yours, arranging and re-arranging them, to create the best balance or flow possible. Some blocks may even need

to be eliminated and one or two new ones constructed if a good finished balance is to be achieved.

I arrange my blocks over a large white sheet or mattress pad which has been fastened to the wall or a drape. If you are short of wall space, work on the floor. The mattress pad, besides being portable, is easy to roll up and tuck away when necessary. You may want to move it to an outside grassy area, patio or driveway. The mattress pad allows you to pin your blocks in position and gives you a neutral background against which to analyze the balance.

Once you have arranged the blocks, step back and squint at the composition to get a better feel of the flow or balance. You can use the two examples above for practice.

The 'poor balance' example shows four dark blocks concentrated at the lower left corner. The top row consists of light colors and patterns with many small points. All the blocks with curves are stacked on the far right side.

Now study the 'good balance' example. The blocks with dark backgrounds have been distributed to the corners and one has been positioned in the center. It is surrounded on two sides by circular moving blocks. The two blocks with light fabrics have been separated and placed opposite each other.

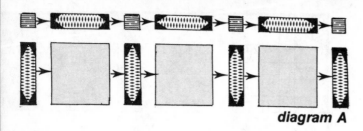

diagram A

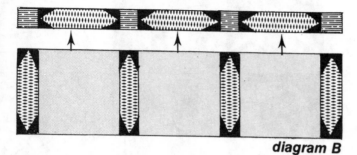

diagram B

patterns

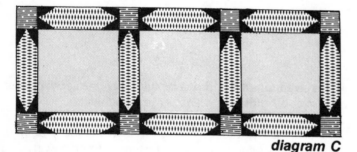

diagram C

diagram D

function of lattice

The fabric strips or sashing, often placed around each block in a sampler, are called lattice. Adding lattice will increase the total size of a top. It also helps set each block apart, framing it, thus allowing each block to be appreciated individually. In addition, it unifies the blocks which are composed of a variety of designs and colors. The lattice's ability to give a sense of harmony often determines the final feeling of balance and flow necessary to a good sampler.

I have designed four different lattice patterns for this book and suggest you try one of them with your sampler. Examples of the four patterns are shown on the sampler quilts pictured on pages 45 through 52.

use of color and print

Consider using solid colors for the lattice if you plan to do extensive quilting in this area as the stitches will be seen at their best. Each lattice pattern will look entirely different when different solid colors or when printed fabrics are used. Study the color plates on pages 45 through 52 and read the section on print and color, pages 2 through 4 for additional ideas.

assemblying sequence

Diagrams A through D show the assemblying sequence for lattice. I prefer to lay all the pieces out in front of me, usually on the floor. This makes it easier to join the pieces in their correct sequence and to sew the right edges into seams. Rows of lattice are assembled, then their seams pressed to one side. The blocks are sewn together in rows with alternating strips of lattice, again pressing the seams carefully.

machine sewing

The sewing machine is the best tool for joining the lattice and sampler blocks once they are **carefully pinned** together. Select a color of thread to blend with the various fabrics and set the machine for 16 stitches per running inch (2,5cm). This close stitch helps prevent the thread from showing on the right side of your work.

Make sure each block is clean, pressed, and squared as described on page 71. Careful pinning and piecing of each seam will help assure that your top has well matched corners and seams.

When joining long rows as in diagram B, pin the rows at each crossing seam, then use additional pins to ease in any fullness. If one row is just a little longer, the fullness can be eased in but if it is very much longer, you may need to repiece some of the crossing seams.

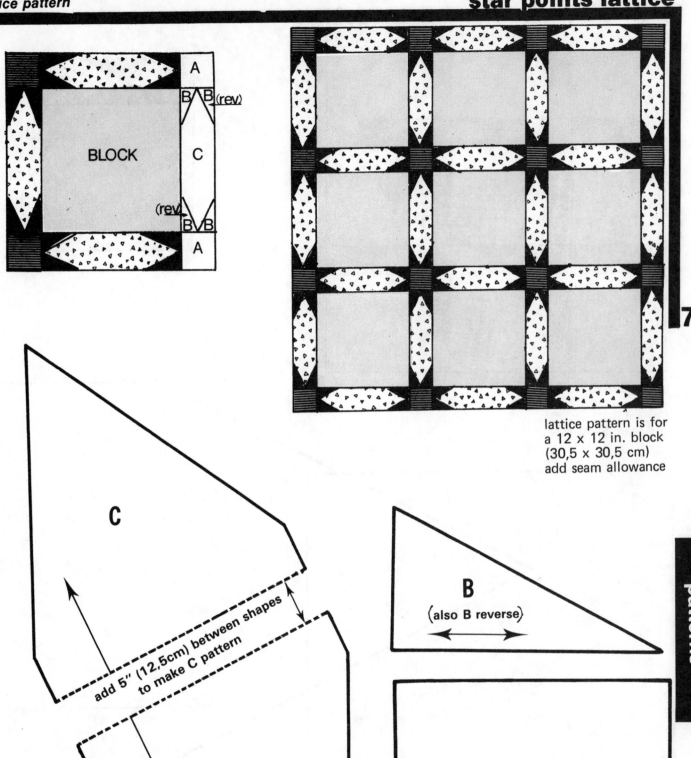

A

B | B (rev)

C

(rev)

B | B

A

BLOCK

73

lattice pattern is for
a 12 x 12 in. block
(30,5 x 30,5 cm)
add seam allowance

C

add 5" (12,5cm) between shapes
to make C pattern

B

⟨also B reverse⟩

A

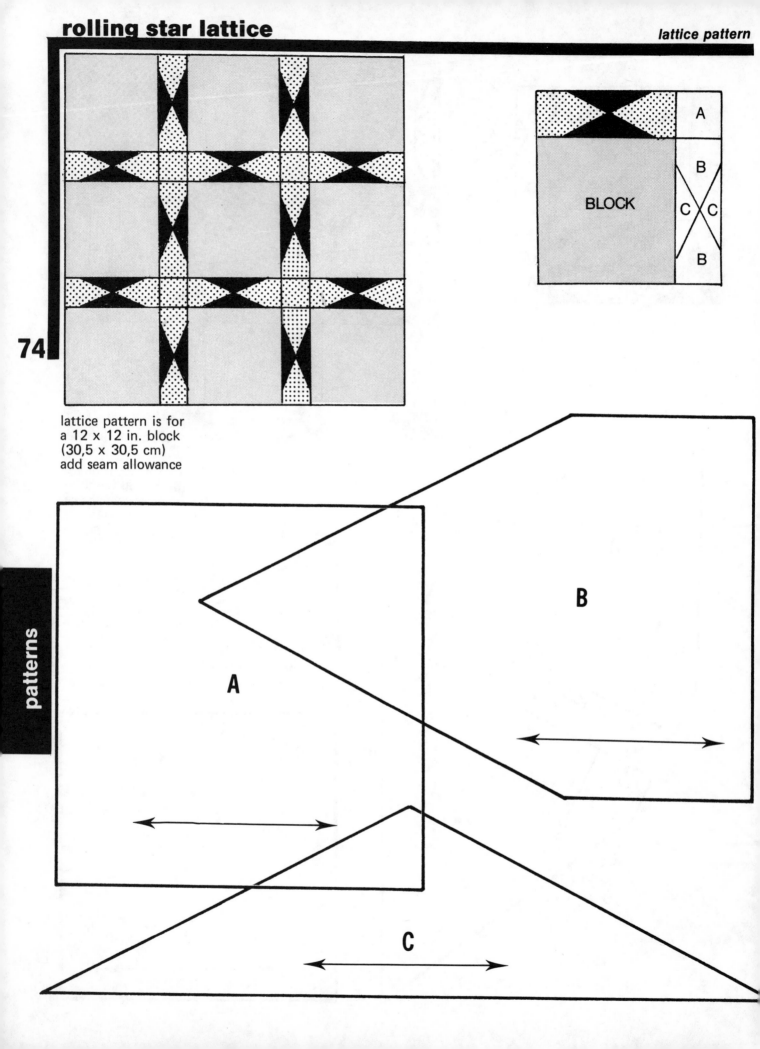

A

BLOCK

B

C

C

B

74

lattice pattern is for
a 12 x 12 in. block
(30,5 x 30,5 cm)
add seam allowance

B

A

C

patterns

ribbon delight lattice

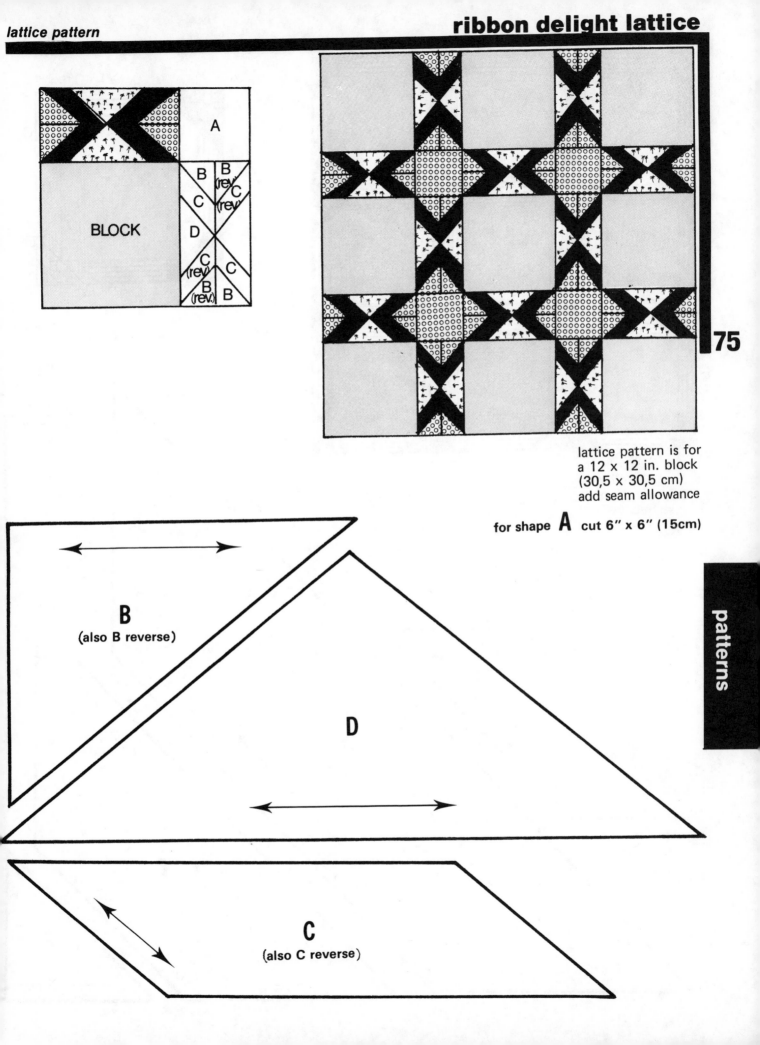

A
BLOCK
B
B (rev.)
C
C (rev.)
C
D
C (rev.)
C
B (rev.)
B

75

lattice pattern is for
a 12 x 12 in. block
(30,5 x 30,5 cm)
add seam allowance

for shape **A** cut 6" x 6" (15cm)

B
(also B reverse)

D

C
(also C reverse)

patterns

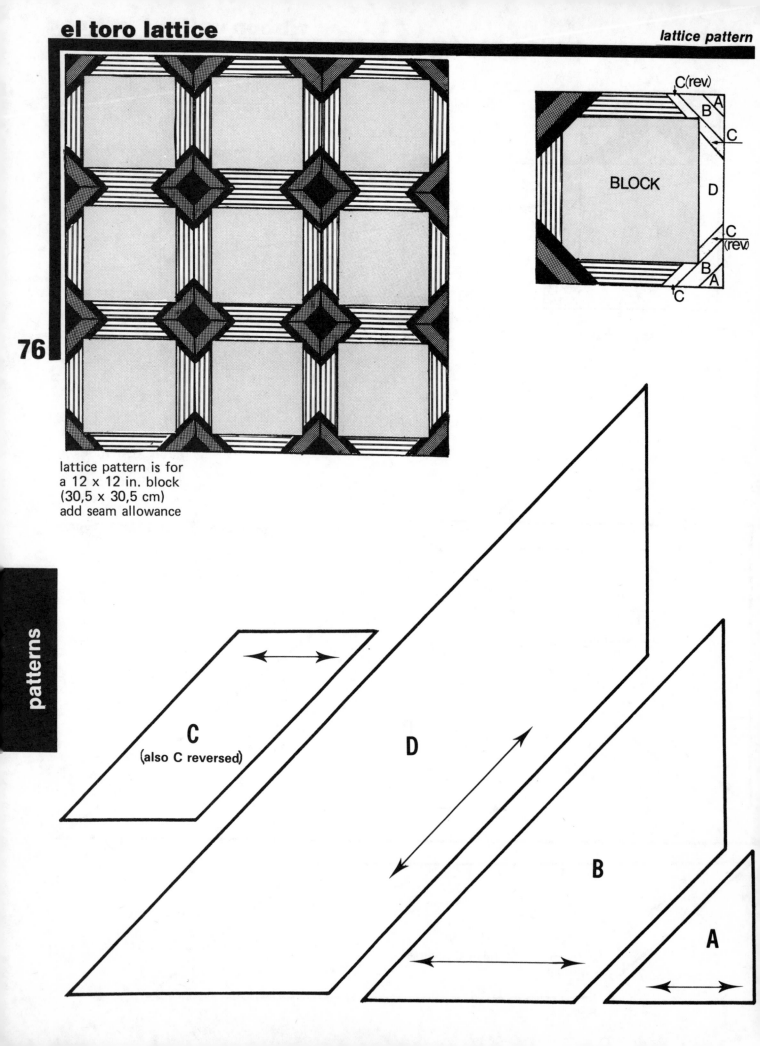

BLOCK

C(rev)
A
B
C
D
C (rev)
B
A
C

76

lattice pattern is for
a 12 x 12 in. block
(30,5 x 30,5 cm)
add seam allowance

patterns

C
(also C reversed)

D

B

A

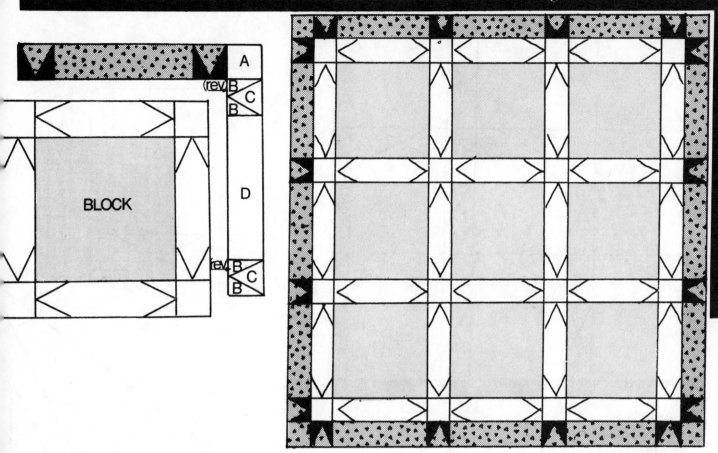

add seam allowance
use with Star Points Lattice

BLOCK

A

(rev) B

C

B

D

B (rev)

C

B

77

for shape **D**

cut 3 x 12 in.

(7,5 x 30,5 cm)

patterns

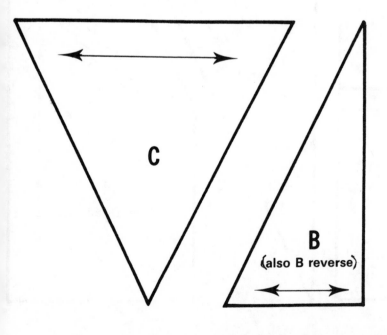

C

B

(also B reverse)

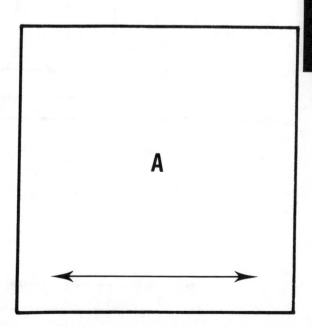

A

rolling star border

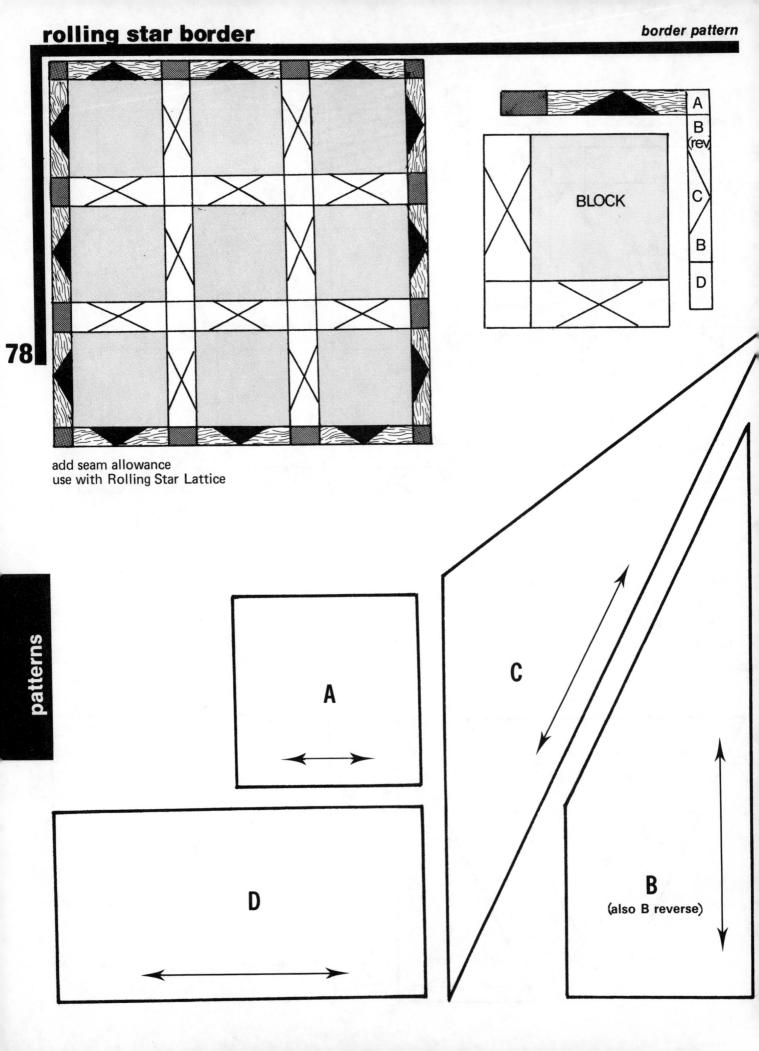

add seam allowance
use with Rolling Star Lattice

BLOCK

A
B
(rev)
C
B
D

patterns

78

A

D

C

B
(also B reverse)

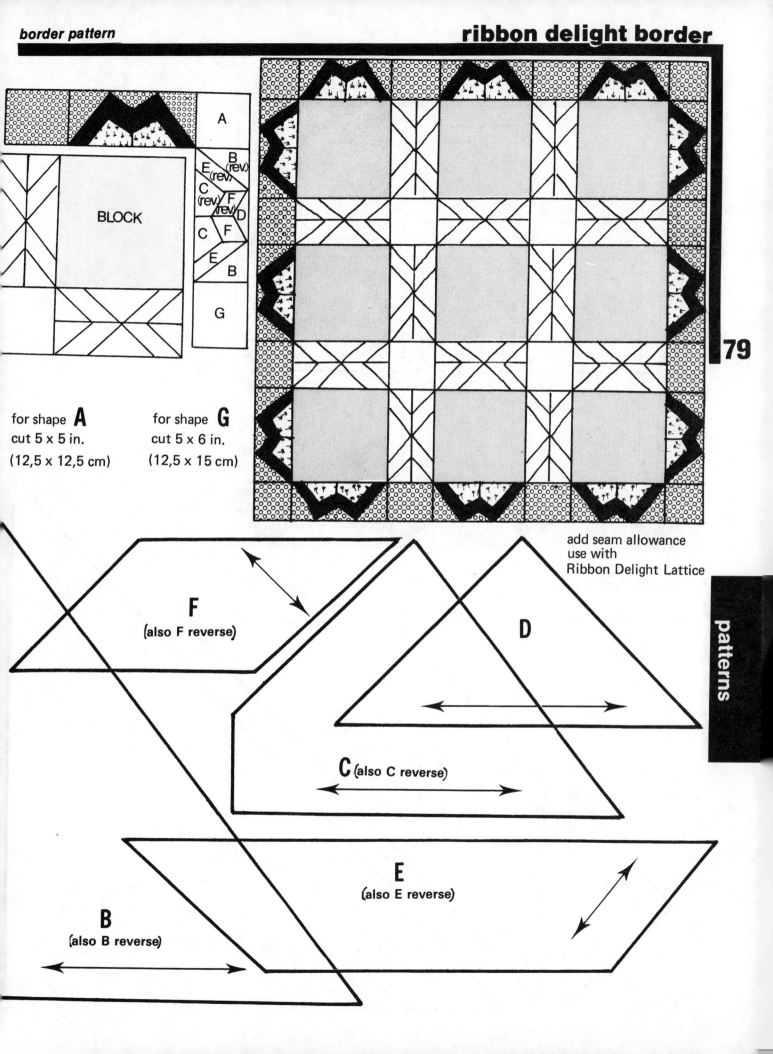

BLOCK

A

B (rev.)

E (rev.)

C (rev.)

F (rev.)

D

F

C

E

B

G

for shape **A**
cut 5 x 5 in.
(12,5 x 12,5 cm)

for shape **G**
cut 5 x 6 in.
(12,5 x 15 cm)

79

add seam allowance
use with
Ribbon Delight Lattice

patterns

F
(also F reverse)

D

C (also C reverse)

E
(also E reverse)

B
(also B reverse)

80

add seam allowance
use with El Toro Lattice

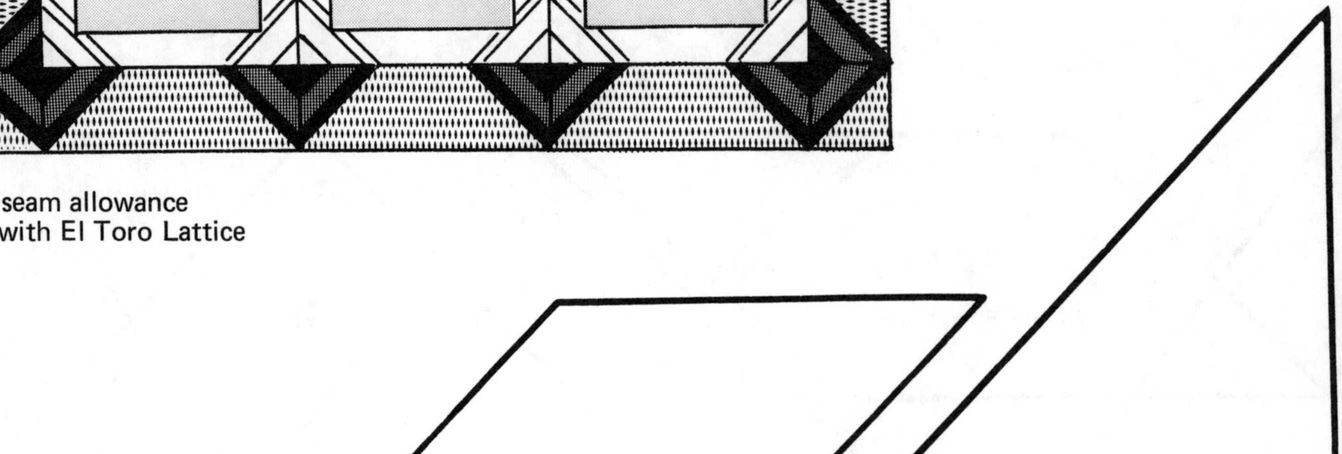

patterns

A

B

D

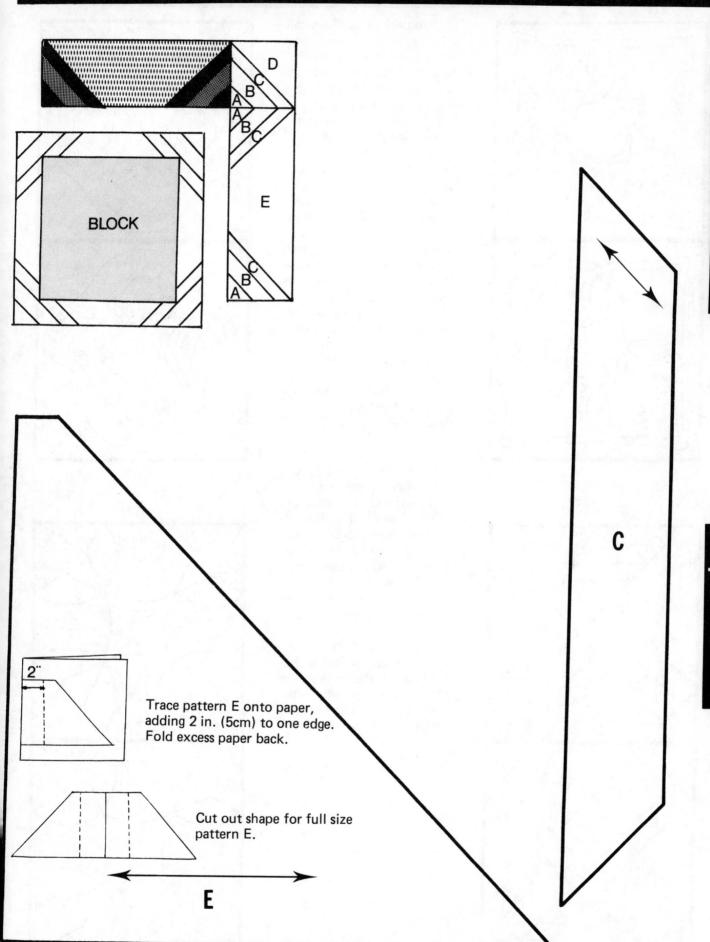

D

C

B

A
A
B
C

E

BLOCK

C
B
A

C

2"

Trace pattern E onto paper,
adding 2 in. (5cm) to one edge.
Fold excess paper back.

Cut out shape for full size
pattern E.

E

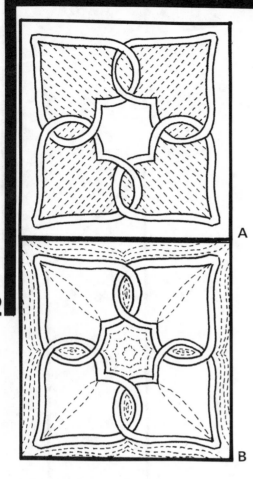

A

B

Quilting refers to the small stitches sewn through and joining the layers of a quilt. It serves to give added strength to the finished item and helps prevent shifting of the layers. It gives additional design interest, texture, and depth which are most important for a wall quilt.

I prefer to let the block suggest the quilting pattern and always draw several different but suitable designs for each block. The drawings on this page show how this can be done. I like to use graph paper to draw my block, then make several copies with a copy machine or carbon paper. Sometimes I outline around the design within the block to see what pattern develops. This was done in examples B, D, E, and H.

Keep in mind that blocks with curving designs, such as the applique blocks, are usually most effective enhanced with straight line quilting as in examples A, E, and G. At the same time, straight, even patchwork will be complimented by curved quilting as shown in example C.

Quilt a shape found within the block as shown in example F. The flower within the applique is used as the quilt design in the corners.

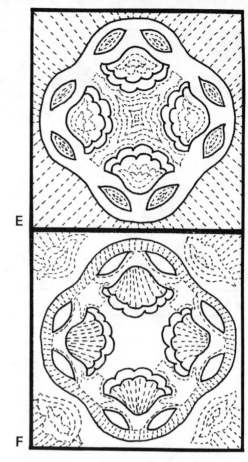

E

F

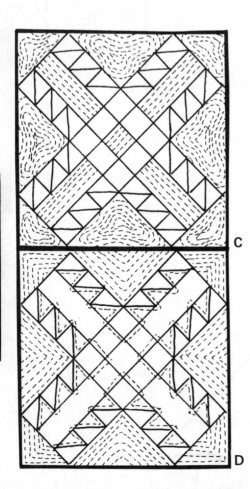

C

D

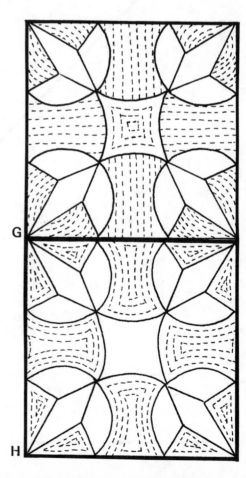

G

H

drawing your own pattern

Filler quilting serves to secure the layers of the quilt and add texture. It also gives a unifying style to the surface; this is especially desirable when combining pieced blocks with applique. Use a ruler or draw freehand for curves.

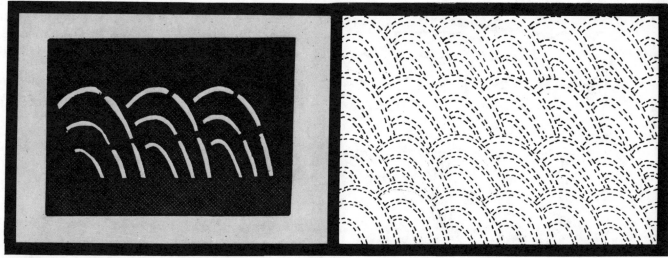

using a purchased pattern

Commercially manufactured patterns or stencils are readily available at most quilt shops and through mail order sources. Many of these stencils can be arranged to provide a filler pattern.

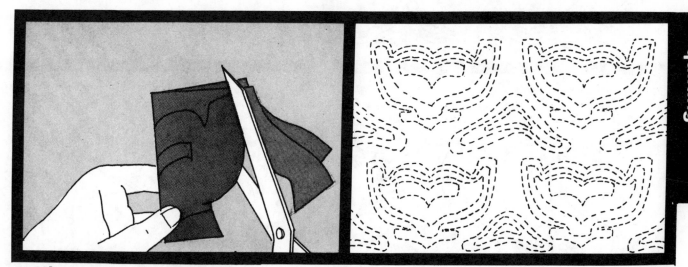

cutting your own pattern

I often make my own stencils from lightweight tagboard, folding it, then drawing a shape out from the fold, around and back to the fold. Make several shapes and select the best one. Design additional lines for quilting, inside and outside the shape.

quilt patterns - designing borders and clusters

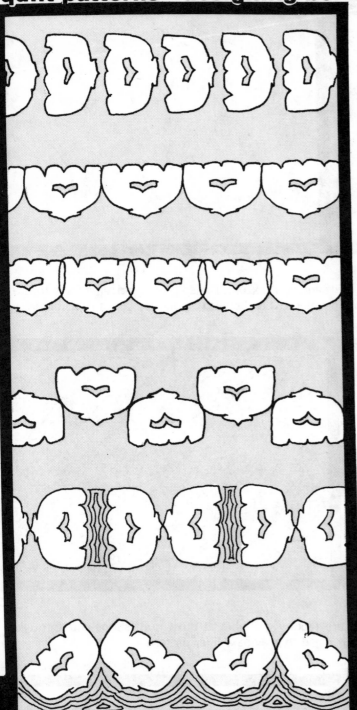

I always study my assembled top, looking at the fabrics and their prints to see if they can suggest a simple shape to develop. There might be an interesting flower that could be elongated or pulled into a swooping curve if the stem were changed. More leaves could be added or new rounded tips could be added to the petals. Perhaps the flower could turn back on itself, or three flowers might form a scroll, a half or full circle. On page 82, you will see how in example F.

Another approach might be studying the negative space or the background areas that are produced by the block. Is there an interesting shape there that could be elaborated on and used in the border?

With imagination and practice you can learn to cut simple shapes from paper as previously described on page 83. I generally cut five to eight shapes and choose one that seems to blend with the feeling of the blocks or the total top. Once I have a suitable shape, I chain it to form a row, overlap it, tilt or twist it, even lay it on its side. The six borders to the left were developed using those techniques.

Additional quilting lines can be added inside and/or outside the shape, lending texture, depth and beauty to the finished design.

The same simple shape can be used for designing clusters or larger units to quilt.

quilting

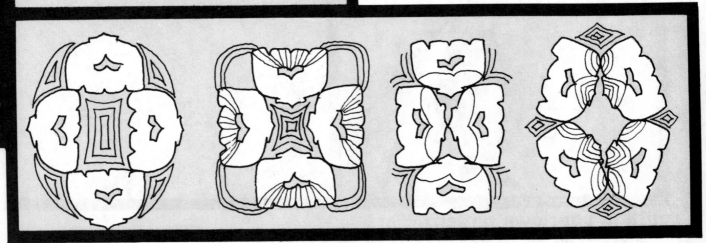

85

Corners need special attention when quilting patterns are being designed for them. The quilting design needs to flow or move around the corner, not end abruptly as in the drawing below.

I usually start my border design at the corner and work out, stretching or shortening the design by small increments. This allows the design to move smoothly with the border, eliminating gaps or empty spaces between the units.

poorly executed corner

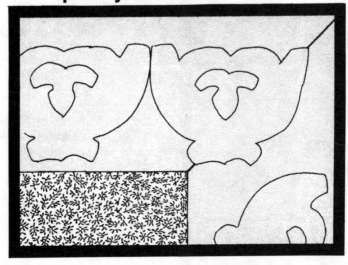

quilting

quilting

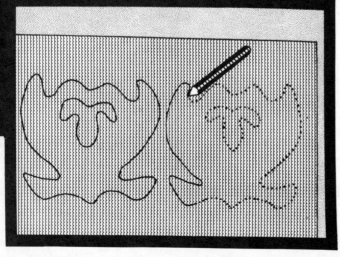

tracing around a stencil

Method 1—Various techniques are available to transfer your quilting design to the quilt top. Position the stencil on the right side of the top. Trace lightly with a sharp no. 2 lead pencil or use a white pencil on dark fabrics. After quilting, light pencil markings will usually not show. They can be easily removed by washing or dry cleaning when the quilt is finished. If you plan to use water soluble marking pens for the tracings, test them first on your fabrics. Sometimes their markings will disappear before you have time to quilt. Never use an iron or soap on blue pen markings as this often sets them.

using dressmaker's carbon

Method 2—Original designs can be drawn onto a sheet of paper, then pinned in place against the right side of the top. Dressmaker's carbon is slipped between the pattern and the top, its right side facing down. Trace along the design lines using a worn out ball point pen. Repeated tracings with a pencil or tracing wheel will cause the paper to tear. I tie a ribbon around the worn out ball point pen to identify it in my supply box. Be sure to test all dressmaker's carbon on your fabrics to see if it is removable—many are not.

dusting through a perforated pattern

Method 3—An original design can be made into a stencil by sewing along the lines with an unthreaded sewing machine. Use a large needle and set the machine for six stitches per running inch (2,5cm). Rub fine sandpaper across the back side of the pattern to clean and open the punctured holes. Position the pattern against the right side of the fabric top. Make a dusting pad using cheesecloth filled with cinnamon, cornstarch, or powdered chalk. Powdered chalk is made by grinding chalk sticks in a blender. Pat over the pattern with the dusting pad.

connecting dusting marks

When you carefully remove the stencil, small dots of dust will be left. Connect the dusting marks with a pencil. Proceed to dust and mark the next area.

working with glass surface

I prefer this method because I use my living room glass top coffee table as a lightbox. Its large surface supports the top I'm working on and allows me to see and position large areas at one time. If I have to stay within the confines of my workroom, I use a lightbox. You can make one using a cardboard box covered with a sheet of glass. Mask the edges of the glass so you don't cut yourself or your quilt top by accident. Tape your stencil onto the glass using masking tape.

tracing onto fabric

Position a lamp or light bulb in an extension cord under the glass or table top. Place your quilt top, right side up over the stencil or shape. Trace lightly onto the top using a sharp no. 2 lead pencil or use a white pencil for dark fabrics.

additional tracings

The fabric top can be moved or repositioned over the stencil as many times as needed to do all the tracings.

working with larger pattern

An original or large pattern can be taped to the glass surface with masking tape. I trace over the pattern with a fine pointed black, felt-tipped pen, which makes it easier to see the lines when the fabric top is in position. Place your fabric top over the glass and trace onto its right side as previously described.

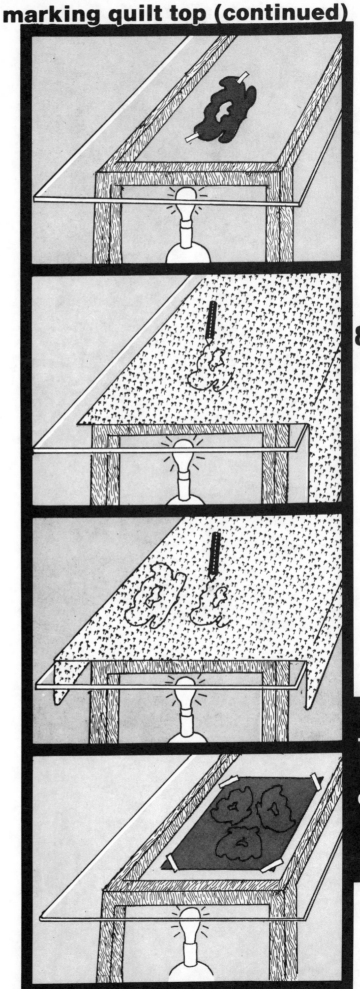

87

quilting

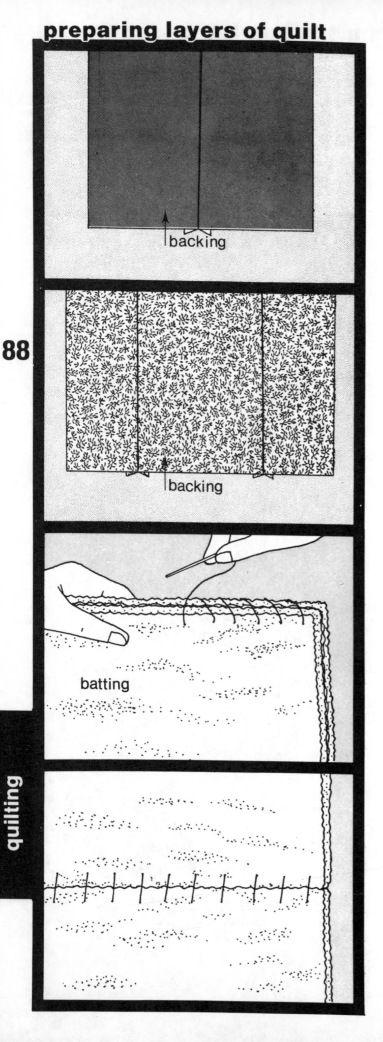

backing with center seam

Choose a fabric for the back of your quilt that will be compatible in color with the top. Your quilting will not show up as obviously on a printed surface which may or may not be desirable.

Bed sheets, while a good buy, have a close thread count making it difficult to quilt through them. I use a needle to test the ease of stitching on all fabrics I am considering.

Most backing will need to be seamed to make it large enough. Sew the seam vertically down the center back.

backing with two seams

If additional seaming is needed, space the seams so they are evenly balanced. Press all seams open.

The backing should be prepared several inches larger than the top.

piecing sheet batting

The batting, like the backing, should be several inches larger than the top.

I prefer a thin bonded sheet batting of polyester which, although it has some fiber migration, holds its loft. A bonded cotton batting, on the other hand, has less fiber migration but less loft.

To piece sheet batting, trim edges to be joined so they are smooth and straight. Holding the two pieces together, use a lacing or whip or overcasting stitch. Quilting thread works well for this.

batting opened flat

The lacing stitches are about 1 in. (2,5cm) apart and ½ in. (1,3cm) deep into the batting. The pieced sheet batting, when pulled open, will lay flat and smooth, its edges butted.

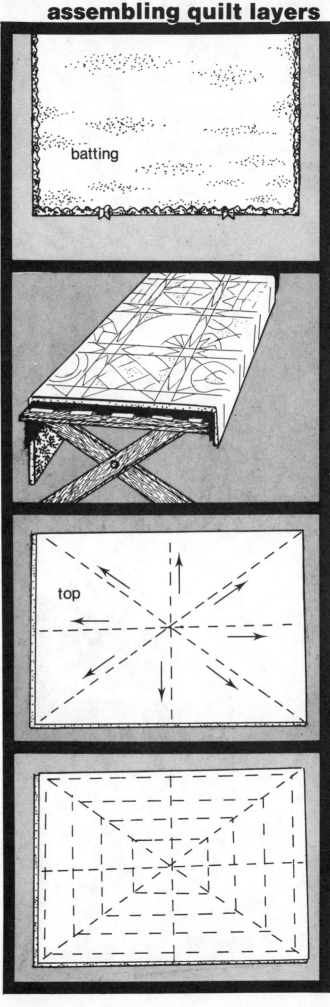

layering backing & batting

After pre-shrinking and pressing the backing fabric, place it wrong side up. If there are any seams, they should be pressed open and showing. Position the sheet batting over the backing and smooth out any lumps or ridges.

work over plastic covered table top

Cover a picnic table or card tables placed in a row with a sheet of plastic or painter's plastic drop cloth. Secure plastic with masking tape. Place the backing and batting over the table, then carefully position the top right side up. The weight of the layers falling over the sides of the table will help smooth the top. The edge of the table will provide a straight line to adjust or straighten the layers.

first bastings

The basting process can be speeded by threading many needles with long threads before you begin. Use a thread that blends with the top's fabrics and wax it to prevent tangling, as shown on page 91. A contrast thread can leave colored fibers in your top.

Baste through the three layers using large stitches, 3 to 4 in. (7,5 to 10 cm) long. Beginning at the center, baste horizontally, then vertically, and finally diagonally.

additional rows

Additional rows are added in concentric rings placed about 5 in. (12,5cm) apart. Once in a while, check the quilt's underside to see that the backing fabric has not gathered during the basting. I give an occasional pull on the back to eliminate this.

When the layers are well basted, pull the backing, which was cut larger, up and over the top, enclosing the edges. This keeps them from fraying while being handled.

hoop resting on lap

An oval or round quilting hoop about 23 in. (58,5cm) in diameter is needed to keep the layers of your quilt stretched taut. I like to work with a hoop supported against the edge of a table or pillow, allowing me the freedom to use both hands for quilting.

Because a hoop is flexible and can be given a quarter or half turn, you can keep your line of quilting always in front of you. For a beginner or average quilter, this is important as it is hard to quilt around corners and away from yourself.

hoop in a stand

Many shops or mail order sources offer quilting hoops with a stand. The inner ring of the hoop fastens to the stand giving you the option to use the legs when quilting at home, or remove the hoop and quilt 'on the go.'

supporting edge of quilt

When quilting close to the outside edge or border, your quilt will need additional support. Strips of twill tape wrapped around the hoop and pinned to the quilt are a quick and flexible solution.

supporting corner of quilt

Strips of twill tape can be attached around the corners in the same manner. When placing your quilt into the quilting hoop, pull the basted layers evenly in all directions to eliminate the possibility of stitching wrinkles into your work.

preparing thread

Select as short a needle as possible when hand quilting; it will help you make shorter stitches. I prefer a 'quilting' or 'between' needle, size 8 or 10.

Cut and wax a short or 18-in. (46cm) length of thread. Longer thread will only twist or tangle by being repeatedly pulled through the layers. You can also use quilting thread which is prewaxed with resin. It is available in a limited range of colors. Sometimes I quilt with a matching thread; other times I prefer a contrasting color. The choice is up to you.

first stitch

Make a small knot as shown on page 9. Insert the needle through the top and into the batting, coming up at the position where you want to start quilting. Notice that you don't stitch through to the backing.

hiding knot

Give the thread a light tug and the knot will pop into the batting or middle layer. Don't pull using the needle but grasp the thread between your fingers. You are now ready to quilt. Page 93 will explain this technique.

quilting stitch.

The number of stitches per running inch will depend on your skill, the weight of the fabric and the thickness of the batt. The thinner the batt the finer you will be able to make your stitches. I try to take five to seven stitches per inch (2,5cm), meaning five to seven stitches showing on the top and the same number showing on the bottom. Work to get your stitches short, neat, uniform and well spaced along the top and bottom. Remember that large stitches will have a greater chance to snag, wear, or break over a period of use.

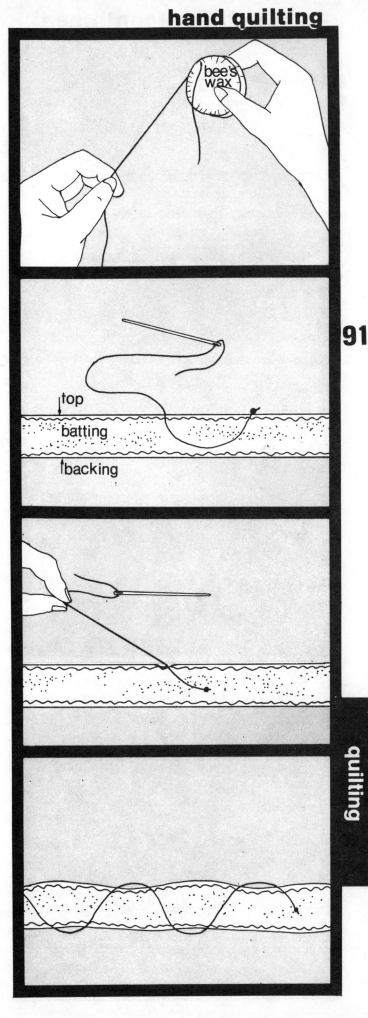

92

finishing your quilting

The finishing knot, just like the beginning knot, should not show on either the top or bottom surface. Be sure to stop quilting and make the knot before you run too short of thread. You will learn to guage this with practice. Bring the needle out of the top and wrap it three or four times as if you were making a French knot.

take last stitch

Slide the wraps close together near the tip of the needle. Insert the needle through the top and batting as though you were taking one more stitch. Hold the end of the thread down with your thumb and forefinger to keep the wraps tight.

needle up - off to the side

Bring the needle up at a slight distance off to the side and away from your quilting line. Notice that this last stitch did not go through the back of the quilt. The knot should be firm, resting on the quilt top; the needle and excess thread are pulled completely through to the top.

hide knot

Tug on the thread and the knot will pop down into the layers, parking itself out of sight. Pull gently again on the thread and cut it at the same time close to the quilt top. When the thread relaxes, the tail will pop through the top and rest in the middle layer.

With knots parked in the batting, there will be no loose threads and your quilting stitches will not work loose even with repeated washings or rugged wear.

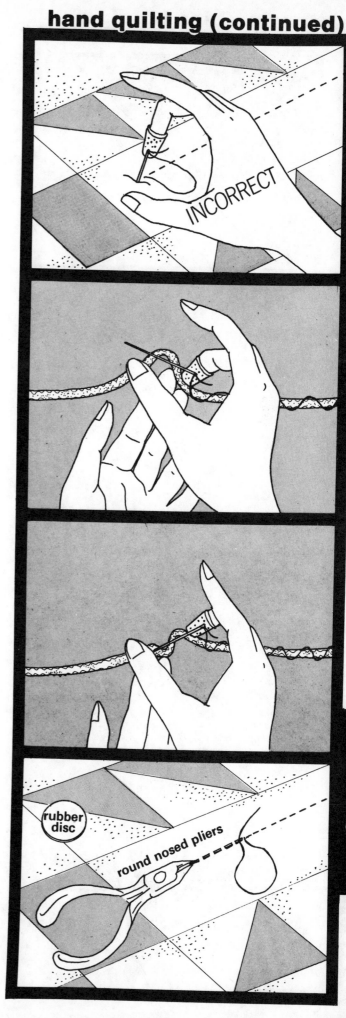

quilting stitch - top view

Right handed people generally quilt right to left and slightly towards the left shoulder. Left handed people work left to right.

Do not poke the needle through the layers using the end of the thimble like a hammer. The needle should be held at its midpoint between the thumb and index finger of the sewing hand. The eye of the needle is set into the side of the thimble. Place the nonsewing hand under the quilt, its index or middle finger against the quilting line.

quilting stitch - working up

As soon as you feel the needle underneath, position the thumb of the sewing hand one to two inches (2,5 to 5 cm) ahead, along the quilting line. Push up with the non-sewing hand against the quilt and down with the thumb of the quilting hand.

additional stitches

Continue this rocking motion, putting additional stitches onto the needle. Concentrate on your stitches, watching to see that you don't guide the needle off to the side of your marked line. At first you may be able to take only one or two stitches onto the needle. That is all right. Practice for a while, then check the back to see if the stitches on the under side are the same length as on the top. Then practice some more.

easing stubborn stitches

If the needle becomes stuck, it can be pulled through to the top using quilting pliers, which are small round nosed pliers found in well stocked hardware stores. A rubber balloon, rubber disc, or gripper will also help you pull through a stubborn needle.

Glance up once in a while to relieve eye strain. Relax and enjoy quilting. The more you practice the better your quilting will become.

finding true bias

I prefer to bind my quilts with my own bias binding rather than straight-grain binding. It's easier to work with and assures you a smooth, ripple-free edge. To find the true bias of your yardage, fold one cut edge over to meet the selvage. The resulting fold is the true bias.

fold fabric again

Pull the top corner, A, back over your yardage to make a second fold. Mark the width of the strips using a ruler. I like to cut 2½-in. (6,5cm) bias and sew it on using ¼-in. (6mm) seams. Allowing for ease, my finished binding is usually ¾ in. (2cm) to 1 in. (2,5cm) wide. Experiment and decide what width you prefer.

seaming bias strips

The bias strips are placed right sides together and then all machine seamed at one time. Press the seams open.

double bias binding

The finished edge of a quilt will have a rolled appearance if it is made from a double bias. Sometimes I add a strip of soft sheet batting to make the binding round out more. The double layers also help prevent shadowing from the quilt top.

A double bias cut is twice as wide as a regular bias strip. Fold it in half and stitch along the two raw edges.

Double bias has the additional advantage of wearing better because of the extra layer of material.

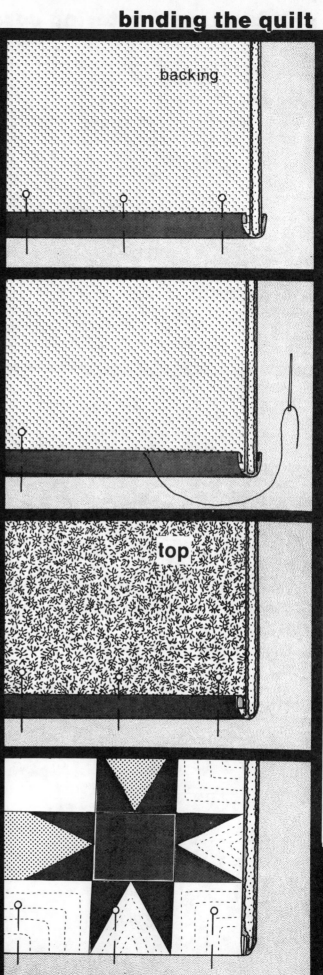

binding with bias

Place the bias binding against the quilt's top, right sides together and pin every 3 in. (7,5cm). Otherwise, the long strip of bias will tend to stretch. Machine sew using a ¼-in. (6mm) seam allowance. Miter the corners as you reach them using the double miter technique described on page 97.

Pull the binding to the back side, turning under a ¼-in. (6mm) hem. Pin in place.

hem binding

Use a hemming or blind stitch to sew the back side of the binding into place. Select a close matching thread. Sew from the folded edge of the bias placing your stitches ¼ in. (6mm) apart, or closer.

self-binding

This binding needs to be planned in advance because the backing must be large enough to fold over the quilt's edge and form a binding on the top. Turn under a ¼-in. (6mm) hem, and sew in place with a blind stitch. To miter the corners, see page 96.

knife edge finish

This edging is done by turning under a narrow hem along both the backing and the top. The batting will need to be trimmed out of the way and should end at the turned under raw edge of the backing hem. Pin in place. You can sew the knife edge hem by hand using a blind stitch or sew by machine close to the quilt with the top surface facing up.

finishing technique

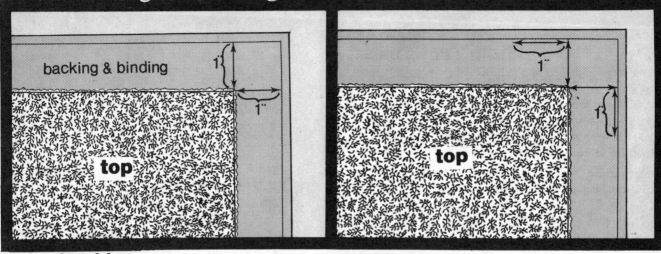

trim backing

The backing which becomes a self-binding should extend beyond quilt top 1-1/4 in. (3,2cm). Draw 1/4 in. (6mm) seam allowance along edges.

measure

Make measurements as shown.

96

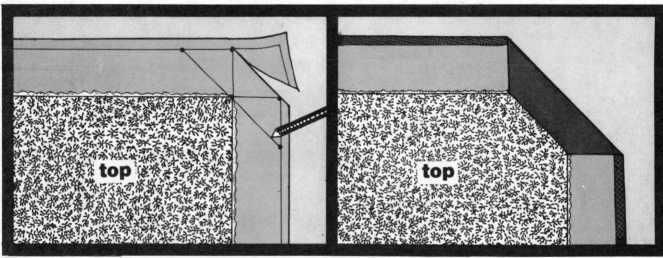

trim corner

Connect marks, trim off outside corner.

fold corner in

Fold under seam allowance. Fold trimmed corner over top as shown.

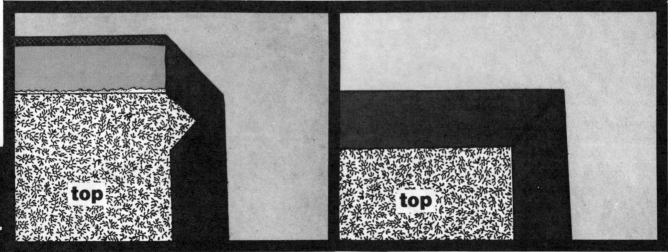

fold edge in

Fold one side in, then other side. Using a blind stitch, sew down edges and mitered corner. The finished binding is 1 in. (2,5cm) wide.

hem

Follow the same directions but change the measurements accordingly for a wider or narrower binding. Example—a 2-in. (5cm) finished binding requires 2¼ in. (5,7cm).

finishing technique

measuring for corner

With right sides together and quilt top facing up, machine stitch ¼ in. (6mm) from edge. Stop ½ in. (1,3cm) before corner where seam lines meet. Machine backstitch and cut thread.

fold binding back

Using a pencil and ruler, draw seam allowance of ¼ in. (6mm) and measurements shown in first diagram. This will give you a 1-in. (2,5cm) finished binding. Fold binding back.

97

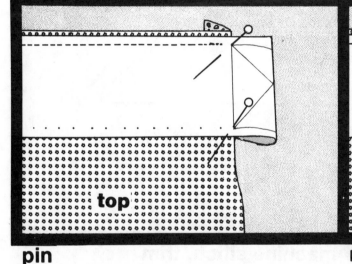

pin

Pin the binding back, checking the back side to see that the pins emerge at the same position. Notice that the quilt top is pulled back out of the way.

machine stitch, trim

Using 20 stitches per inch (2,5cm) machine sew starting at top pin working to the point then down to the bottom pin. Do not sew into the ¼-in. (6mm) seam allowance. Trim excess fabric away.

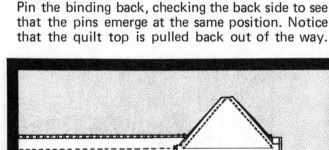
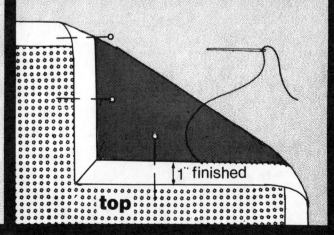

sew on binding

Position and pin binding along next edge, pulling mitered corner out of the way. Machine sew binding to quilt, starting exactly where you left off. Pivot at corner and sew along next side. Repeat process.

finish back side

Pull binding over to the back side, turning under ¼-in. (6mm) seam allowance. Pin in place and sew with small blind stitches.

finishing technique

border with mitered corner

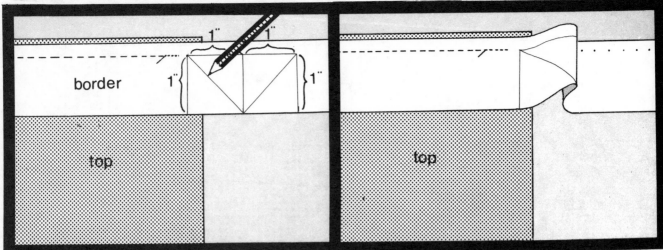

measuring for corner

With right sides together and quilt top facing up, machine sew ¼ in. (6mm) from cut edge. Stop ½ in. (1,3cm) before corner where seam lines meet. Machine backstitch, raise presserfoot and cut thread.

fold border fabric back

Using a pencil and ruler, draw seam allowance ¼ in. (6mm) and measurements shown in first diagram. This will give you a 1-in. (2,5cm) finished border. Fold border fabric back.

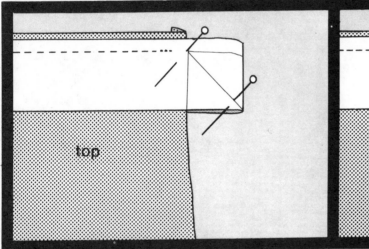

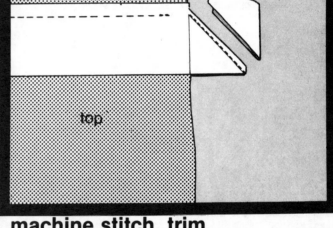

pin

Pin the border fabric, checking the back side to see that the pins emerge at the same position. Notice that the quilt top is pulled back out of the way.

machine stitch, trim

Using 20 stitches per inch (2,5cm) machine sew from top pin diagonally along line off bottom edge. Trim excess fabric away.

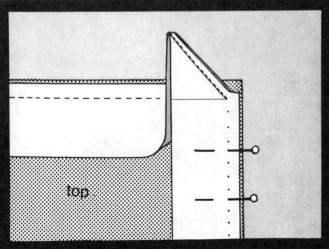

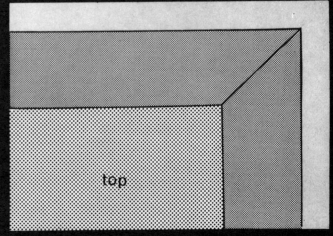

sew to next edge

Position and pin border along next edge, pulling mitered corner out of the way. Machine sew border to quilt, starting where you left off. Pivot at corner and sew down next side. Repeat process.

finished corner

Press seam of mitered corner open. This gives a finished border width of 1 in. (2,5cm). To make a wider or narrower border, repeat directions but change the measurements accordingly.

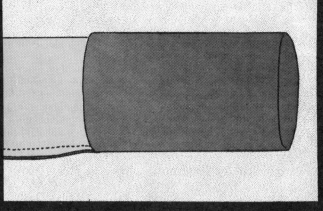

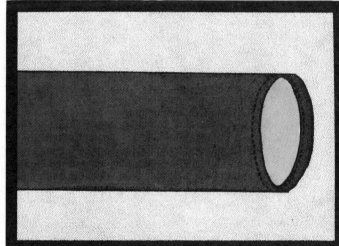

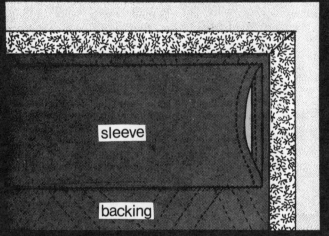

make a casing

Using the same fabric as the quilt's backing, cut a strip 1 in. (2,5cm) wider than the distance across your quilt's backing and 7 in. (18cm) long. Fold, sewing right sides together.

turn right side out

Pull the fabric right sides out.

finish ends

Turn the raw edges of the ends under ¼ in. (6mm), then turn under again. Sew in place by hand or machine.

sleeve stitched into place

Sew the sleeve across the top backside of the quilt, leaving a slight fullness or bubble extending outward. Sew using a blind stitch.

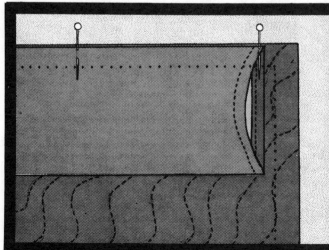

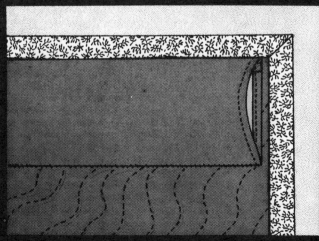

2nd technique

The sleeve can also be pinned onto the quilt's backing before the quilt is bound.

2nd technique - finished

When the binding is sewn onto the quilt, the stitching will also catch the top of the sleeve. Hand hem the bottom edge.

patterns in alpabetical order

100

index

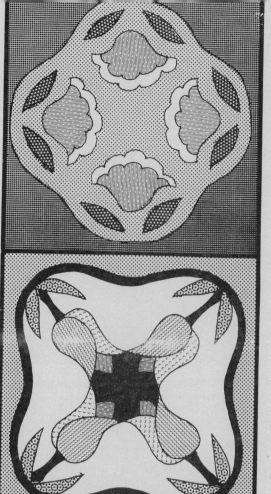
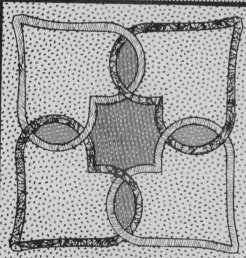